Praise For

This Is Your Life, Not A Dress Rehearsal

"In This Is Your Life, Not A Dress Rehearsal, Jim Donovan has put together a magnificent 'success manual' that is down to earth, fun to read, and right on target. Read and apply Jim's proven success principles and you will achieve extraordinary results in your life!"

Jeff Keller, Author,
The Monthly Motivator

"Once again, you've assembled basic truths to share with the world. Your newest contribution is so supportive, like an unconditional friend. It's here to inspire, to nurture, to encourage and to offer hope. 'This is Your Life.' is a powerful companion and must reading."

Bonnie Ross–Parker, Senior Executive,
The Peoples Network

"Because of the wisdom in This Is Your Life, Not A Dress Rehearsal, fewer people will die with their music still in them. Donovan's ideas work because he takes 'Grow where you're planted' to an energized new level, teaching people how to have the courage to realize their biggest dreams and truly live their version of the good life. Use Jim's book to help you realize every dream you've ever dared to dream and more."

Barbara Garro,
Business Talk

"God said, 'Build a better world,' and that's exactly what you are accomplishing with this wonderful book. Congratulations!"

DAVID HANDLEMAN, INROADS, INC.,
BUSINESS CONSULTANT

"This book is power perfect!. When the student is ready . . . Thank you, thank you."

CAROL ROTH, INDEPENDENT SENIOR SALES DIRECTOR,
MARY KAY COSMETICS

"I'm delighted that a motivational work combining lifestyle and financial growth principles is available in a single, concisely written, well balanced book."

JAN MOSS, C.E.O.,
WORLD WITHOUT WALLS, INC.

"Sometimes we need to talk to someone who will give us a word of support, an inspirational example, a life changing principle by which to set a new course, or a kick in the pants. In his book, This Is Your Life, Not A Dress Rehearsal, Jim Donovan does all of this, and more. This book is an essential small business resource."

JIM BLASINGAME,
THE SMALL BUSINESS ADVOCATE

THIS IS

YOUR

LIFE,

NOT A DRESS

REHEARSAL

PROVEN PRINCIPLES FOR CREATING
THE LIFE OF YOUR DREAMS

BY JIM DONOVAN

To Albert

BOVAN PUBLISHING GROUP, INC.
POST OFFICE BOX 1147
BUCKINGHAM, PA 18912

www.jimdonovan.com

ISBN: 0-9650534-2-3

Library of Congress Catalog Card Number: 98–96600

Printed in the United States of America

ACKNOWLEDGEMENTS

To Georgia, my wife and best friend, for all her patience, support and belief in my work and my mission.

To my sister Debbie Donovan for being there when I needed help.

Heartfelt thanks to Nancy and Terry Sibley for their faith in my abilities and belief in my work.

Special thanks to Beth Meninger for sharing her insights and ideas and to Jan Moss for her editorial assistance.

To Catherine Colletta, Lillian Kalfas and Kim Peck for their assistance in the preparation of this book.

To Katherine Glover and Steve Price for their assistance, suggestions, patience, and support of my writing and to Sandee, Kim, Jewel and Chris at INTI Publishing for all their help and encouragement.

I especially want to recognize and thank all of my fellow authors and independent publishers in the Publishers Marketing Association for their selfless sharing of ideas, expertise and information.

Of course, my endless gratitude to all of the great minds who have shared their ideas and experiences so that we all may grow and prosper.

Most of all, I want to thank the many readers of Handbook To A Happier Life and my Jim's Jems newsletter who took the time to write and share their successes with me. It's their dedication to creating a better life that motivates me to be the best I can be. As my friend, Terri Lonier, once said, "We're all in this together."

TABLE OF CONTENTS

INTRODUCTION

"Man was born to live, not to prepare to live."

BORIS PASTERNAK

My story

You may be asking yourself, "What qualifies this guy to write this book?" What qualifies me is that I've been there. I've been to the bottom and back. I sank to some of the lowest points a human being can go — mentally, physically, spiritually, emotionally and financially. I was all the way down, as far down as I ever want to go again. Amazingly, though, as far down as I was, I was able to turn things around and climb back from the devastation that my life had become, all by applying the ideas discussed in this book.

Through a chain of events and circumstances, totally caused by my actions, my life had become a total disaster. I was living in a small, rented room with a shared bathroom in the South Bronx, one of the worst neighborhoods in New York City. I'll never forget the cockroaches. They were so bold they didn't even run when the light was turned on. Instead, they stood there as if to say, "What are you doing in my bathroom?" I was barely able to pay the $45 a week rent. What little money I was earning from day jobs was going to support my drinking habit. I had no friends left because, as a result of my excesses, I had become impossible to be around. My health was failing rapidly due to my lifestyle and poor eating habits. I was spiritually bankrupt, feeling that, for some reason, God had deserted me.

I had, as they say, reached the bottom. I had done it all. Sold my belongings, slept in cars, gone without food for days at a time, been evicted and all the other indignities that are part and parcel to that lifestyle. About the only thing I did not do was panhandle or steal.

I remember one spring evening, walking down Broadway in New York City and, instead of looking at the bright lights and majestic skyline, I was looking at the ground — trying to find a nickel so I would have enough money to buy a pack of cigarettes. There were days when I would walk 20 blocks uptown to 96th street where I could buy loose cigarettes for ten cents each. Talk about walking a mile for a Camel!

The turning point

I finally reached my bottom. I had fallen as low as I could stand. I reached that point where something inside of me said, "This has to change – *now.*" I was fortunate that I had parents who were willing to take me in and give me one more chance. If it were not for them, I would have wound up living in Central Park or worse.

I'm not sure exactly what the turning point was. I know I had taken all the emotional pain I could stand and even thought about taking my own life. My once promising life had become a disaster. I had squandered the talents and gifts I was born with and I made a decision that I had to either change or die. Frankly, at that point in my life, it did not really matter to me which it was.

While I was living in a room in my parents' apartment, I prayed, actually begged, God to do something with me. Not long after that painful time, I found myself in an alcohol treatment program and I was on a path to recovery. At the time, I thought my life was over. I now know it was just beginning.

I received a lot of help and support during my darkest hours. If you are struggling with a serious problem, like addiction, get professional help. Don't try to go it alone. Call a support program, your doctor, minister, priest, rabbi, therapist or someone who is qualified to help in these matters. This is a life and death situation and should not be taken lightly.

I'm not writing this to gain your sympathy or to impress you with my struggle. I'm sharing my story so you can realize that no matter how far down you may have fallen, there is hope.

Most of you reading this book have not, hopefully, gone as far down as I did. Most of you have jobs, houses and families, however, I know you have your challenges too. While your personal situation may not be as dramatic as my experience, it's no less important.

Perhaps you are experiencing financial difficulties. Maybe you're in a dead end job with no future or you're worried about downsizing (that's a modern word for being fired for no apparent reason). Your health may be less than ideal. Perhaps your relationship with your family could use improvement.

Maybe everything is great in your life and you merely want it to be the best it can be. We all want to grow and expand our horizons. There is always more to give and do and have and become. It's human nature to want to experience the best life has to offer.

A simple book

These are simple, practical strategies and techniques that anyone can use. By applying the principles in this book, you can go from wherever you are in your life at this moment, to living a life that is truly the life of your dreams.

Today

Today, many years later, I sometimes pinch myself when I look at the wonderful life I'm living. I thank God everyday for my second chance and I have, as Robert Schuller so aptly put it, "Promised God I will pursue the dream He has given me."

I'm now doing work I love and am having a positive effect on people's lives. I'm totally committed to my work. And I look forward to each new day with excitement and enthusiasm, anxious to begin it. I'm happily married to a wonderful and supportive woman, my wife Georgia, and have a loving family, dear friends and live in a dream home with every luxury I could want, nestled in the woods in beautiful, Bucks County, Pa.

I have more than I ever imagined. But most of all, I'm at peace. I have regained the spiritual connection I felt I had lost. My life has a purpose, as does yours. We are all here to make a contribution that is uniquely ours. We all have our part to play in this drama of life.

Don't just read this book, use it!

Please use this book. Don't merely read it. Apply it. Take from it what you need to make your life everything it can be. Do it now because you deserve it. Do it now because your family deserves the best life possible. Most of all, do it now because this is your life, not a dress rehearsal.

HOW TO USE THIS BOOK

"They can because they think they can."

VIRGIL

How to make the most of this book

If you don't already have a journal, it would be a great idea to get one. It has been said that a life worth living is worth recording. Journals don't need to be elaborate. A simple spiral notebook works just fine. It's like keeping a diary. You just want a place where you can record your thoughts, observations and feelings, a place to write your dreams, your goals and your plans. Many people write in their journals every day, although that's not necessary.

One of the great things about keeping journals is being able to go back through the years. I've been doing this for almost ten years now and I love periodically reading my journals from the years past. It's inspiring to see how far I've come and to realize how many of my dreams have come true. Throughout this book there are exercises. Please do them. Write them in your journal or at least somewhere in a book. As I said earlier, these principles work, but only if you use them.

I suggest you read through the entire book. Then, go back and invest some time doing the exercises. This is where the real benefit lies. You can read all the books ever written but if you don't put the ideas into practice, nothing will change. Most of us already know what to do. The question is are we doing it?

You can change your life

It does not matter where you are starting from or how far down you may have fallen. You can have lifelong success. You can turn your life around from wherever you are. I have been at the bottom. I know how it feels. I also know that you can change your circumstances. I have done it and I have witnessed many others do the same.

Proven principles

The information in this book is not theory. These aren't just a bunch of "nice ideas." They are proven principles that work. These ideas have stood the test of time. I have personally used these ideas and techniques in my own life. They were passed on to me by others and I'm passing them on to you. I have used these ideas to make major changes in my own life. I know they work and I know that if they worked for me, they'll work for you. I have taught these strategies in seminars and workshops and have seen, first hand, the results people produced by applying these simple techniques.

It's up to you

If you want to achieve lifelong success, you can; however, only *you* can do it. I cannot change your life. No book ever written can change your life. In the end, it's up to you.

Don't take what is here on blind faith. Work with the ideas, test them, question them. If something here is in conflict with your belief, leave it. Take only what works for you. This is your life. You deserve for it to be the best you can make it. You deserve to have the life of your dreams. You deserve lifelong success.

Ready, set, succeed!

Fasten your seat belt, for you are about to embark on a ride that can be so incredible, so inspiring, so exciting, so grand, so powerful . . . and it just keeps getting better and better and better. Enjoy your journey and the experiences life has to offer. Begin now to live the life of your dreams.

WHAT ARE YOU WAITING FOR?

"After all is said and done, more is said than done."

ANONYMOUS

Do it now! Whatever it is you have been putting off, do it. This is your life, it's not a dress rehearsal. What is it you have always wanted to do but, for some unknown reason, never quite get around to? I'm referring to those usually minor desires, not major goals like "get married" or "start a business."

For me it has been things like, swim with dolphins and ride in a glider plane. These were not major accomplishments but still, for some reason, I had been putting them off for years. Why? Why is it we have a tendency to treat our lives as though we will live forever?

In truth, our time here on this earth is but a brief moment in time. If you compare our, perhaps, 100 years here to the age of this planet we call home, you will see we are only here for a blink in time.

What are you putting off? What are some of the things you have always wanted to experience but are postponing because you think you have all the time in the world?

Read the obituaries in today's newspaper and realize that everyone whose name is in there thought they had another day. It's not my intent to offend you, but I do want to shock you into the realization that — this is it! This is your life.

Your life is precious

Don't treat your life lightly. Live now! Have you always wanted to sky dive? Visit the Great Pyramids? Swim with dolphins? See Niagara Falls? Whatever it is you have always wanted to do but have been putting off, decide now to do it. Make a plan. Determine what you will need to do to prepare. Find out the costs involved. Take action.

When I started writing this book I had still not experienced flying in a glider plane, even though it was something I really wanted to do. There were no logical reasons why I had not done it. I simply kept putting it off. It was always in my "someday I'll" file.

Someday is now! I'm pleased to say that now, as I'm putting the finishing touches on this book, I *have* experienced the thrill of sailing through the sky in total silence. I decided to take my own advice and make *"someday"* now. It was great! Doing it was simple enough. All I needed to do was take action.

In your journal, answer the following:

What is it you have always wanted to do?

What preparations will you need to make?

What is your target date to complete this?

WHOSE LIFE IS IT ANYWAY?

"Most men die with their music still in them."

RALPH WALDO EMERSON

Whose life are you living? Are you living *your* dream or someone else's?

How much of your life is being decided by someone else? Are you in a profession you dislike because it's expected of you? Do you engage in activities you would rather skip, simply because it's part of your "role" as a father or mother, daughter or son, spouse or friend?

What about you? Doesn't your opinion count? It's not only reasonable but mentally healthy for you to direct your own life.

If you find yourself in a profession you don't especially like, try asking yourself the following question: If I were starting over in my career, what would I choose to do?

Some people retire and, because they can do whatever they want, begin a second career. This time, they do what they love and, many times, become highly successful.

Famous the second time around

You may not remember that Caroll O'Connor, the actor who created the role of Archie Bunker in "All In The Family" and later played the burly police chief in "In The Heat of the Night," was a high school teacher until he was in his forties. While teaching is surely a noble profession, his greatest gifts to humanity were clearly to come from his acting talents. Fortunately, for those of us entertained by his talents, he followed his bliss and became an actor.

Another example of the second career is the comedian Phylis Diller. She was a cleaning lady until she was 37. Incidentally, she was inspired to ignite her unused potential by reading a self-help book, *The Magic of Believing,* by Claude Bristol. Interestingly enough, Liberace, the great pianist, attributed the strategies in this same book to his huge success and enormous wealth.

Take charge of your life

You owe it to yourself to run your own life. I'm not suggesting that you go out and change everything overnight, however, you can begin to direct your life where you would like it to go.

For example, if you have always wanted to be an actress or actor, but have financial responsibilities which require you to work a "real job," you could satisfy your need to act by joining a local theater group. Many a community theater performer works happily at a nine-to-five job Monday through Friday, knowing they have an outlet for their creative selves on the weekend.

If your time is being taken up in the role of wife and mother, you could set aside time for yourself. Time to pursue your other dreams. You could arrange for your spouse to take care of your children while you take care of your own needs.

Taking care of yourself is not selfish. The Bible says we

should love our neighbor as ourselves. It does not say *instead of* or *more than*. Give yourself permission to treat yourself as someone special. Begin to set aside time to do some of the things you want to do for yourself.

If you are in a job you strongly dislike, start devising a plan which will allow you to make a change. Perhaps you need to go for re-training in another profession. I know of several nurses who, when they realized they were spending more time filling out paperwork than caring for patients, began new careers as massage therapists. This gave them the satisfaction of working directly with people.

CHAPTER 1 – ACCEPTANCE & ATTITUDE

"The last of the human freedoms is to choose one's attitude in any given set of circumstances."

VICTOR FRANKL

Years ago, when I lived in New York City, I used to take the subway to work. Usually, there were hundreds of people on the platform waiting for the train. Sometimes, the trains were late for one reason or another and I used to watch as a few of the commuters became anxious and stressed, trying to "make" the train come. We've all seen this type of person. I'll call him "Hyper Harry." Hyper Harry would begin pacing up and down the platform, look at his watch, then lean over and look down the track to see if the train was there. He would continue this ritual of pacing, looking and leaning as if doing this would somehow cause the train to arrive. Meanwhile, his blood pressure was rising and you could see the veins in his neck popping.

I noticed that, no matter how fast Harry paced, the train did not come any sooner. All of his pacing and anxiety had no effect whatsoever on the train. All it did was stress him out. Clearly this was a situation Harry couldn't change. He would have been happier and more at peace if he had simply accepted his powerlessness in the situation. The moral of the story is that, while we cannot change many situations, we can always change how we view it and how it affects us.

How many of you, like Hyper Harry, will allow a situation that is out of your control to cause you emotional turmoil?

Acceptance

Acceptance is the first key to lifelong success. Acceptance means accepting ourselves, our conditions and the world around us as it is, not how we wish it to be. It means getting out of denial and getting honest with ourselves. It means analyzing a situation and accepting that which we cannot control or change. It means having the courage to change those things that are in our power to change. It means being wise enough to know the difference between the two.

There is a wonderful little prayer — the Serenity Prayer — which can remind us to be more accepting:

God grant me the

Serenity to accept the things I cannot change,

Courage to change the things I can,

Wisdom to know the difference.

Denial

When I talk about denial, I'm not talking about the river in Africa (get it–the Nile?). I'm talking about being 50 pounds overweight and rationalizing it by telling yourself you have "big bones." Are your bones really big or are you simply overweight from eating too much and not exercising?

Accept yourself as you are right now – good or bad. Be honest with yourself and acknowledge where you are. I'm not suggesting that you should not consider reducing your weight to a more healthy number. I'm simply suggesting that you must first accept and acknowledge your present condition.

People who have overcome addictions to alcohol, drugs, food or gambling have first learned to admit and accept their problem. This acceptance demonstrates your willingness to "own" the problem which, in turn, gives you the power to change it.

Affirm that you have created your current situation, either consciously or unconsciously, take responsibility for it, and become willing to change.

The more you can accept the reality of what *is* instead of how you *wish* things were, the more you will have taken the first step towards creating a happy and successful life.

Accept yourself

Too many of us have bought into negative self images. The major social problems in our society — drug addiction, alcoholism, crime, teenage gangs, divorce and most others — begin with a poor self image and low self esteem. Most criminals have low self esteem. All you need to do to confirm this is visit a prison and talk to the inmates. The first thing you will notice is that they continually look down at the floor when speaking to you. This is a dead giveaway of a low self image.

During one of my workshops, a woman remarked how she did not like going to events and meeting new people because, as she put it, "Then they will know how dumb I'm." The truth of the matter is that she is a very intelligent person but has developed this negative self image and allowed it to limit her experience.

Louise Hay, the bestselling author, suggests we work with the affirmation, *"I approve of myself."* I urge you to try this for yourself, especially if you have a low self image. If you want to get a quick read on your present level of self esteem, stand in front of a mirror and say aloud, "I approve of myself." Don't be surprised if it makes you uncomfortable, even scared. I have seen people burst into tears doing this exercise. However, if you continue to do this, over time, you will begin to experience changes in how you feel about yourself and in your life in general. Louise suggests you recite, write, sing these words 300–400 times a day!

Practice receiving a compliment with a simple "thank you" instead of brushing them off by saying "its no big deal."

You deserve compliments. You deserve love. You deserve happiness. *Remember, God doesn't make junk!*

It's useful to keep in mind that, while you will never be perfect, you can become a perfect you. Personally, I have always liked the concept that my life is a work of art in progress. Like an artist working on a painting, I can work on different areas of my life. I'm constantly changing, growing and evolving, refining a little at a time. Of course, it will never be fully completed. Life is about changing and growing.

By identifying the areas of your own life you want to change, you are on your way to building lifelong success. Later, we will develop definite plans for making changes, but for now, simply identify what it is you want to change.

To become clearer about the changes you want to make, complete the following exercise.

EXERCISE — ACCEPTANCE

On a sheet of paper, draw six boxes (see example on the next page). Label them as shown, with the six major areas of your life:

- Family/social

- Career

- Health/fitness

- Spiritual/emotional

- Financial

- Mental/educational.

In each box, what it is you would like to change or work on improving? For example, if you are overweight and have health challenges, write that in the box marked "Health/Fitness." If your income is not what you would like it to be, write "increase income" in the "Financial" box.

You will, most likely, have something in each of the boxes. That's OK. Remember, we are all in a constant state of evolving.

ACCEPTANCE

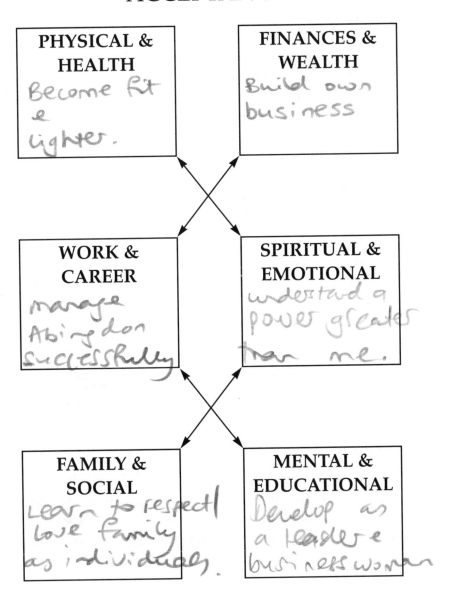

PHYSICAL & HEALTH

Become fit e lighter.

FINANCES & WEALTH

Build own business

WORK & CAREER

manage Abingdon successfully

SPIRITUAL & EMOTIONAL

understand a power greater than me.

FAMILY & SOCIAL

Learn to respect love family as individuals.

MENTAL & EDUCATIONAL

Develop as a leader e businesswoman

Attitude

Another key to lifelong success is Attitude. Your attitude affects everything in your life. How's your attitude? Are you one of those people who is always blaming outside forces for your problems? Do you walk around in a negative state of mind most of the time? I think not. People like that would never have opened this book in the first place.

However positive you may be most of the time, there will be days when you just feel negative. While this may be fine for a brief period, prolonging a negative attitude has disastrous consequences. A negative attitude robs your initiative and destroys your discipline.

The "so what" or "who cares" attitude stops you from taking the actions that will help you build the kind of life you want to have for yourself and your family.

Your attitude determines your altitude.

What happens

Here's how a negative attitude robs us of our potential for good. At one of the low points in my own life, I had developed a "who cares, what's the use" attitude. I felt that I was stuck where I was because of circumstances outside my control and blamed the world for my conditions. I figured I was at the bottom, so why even care? The problem is, as I learned through a lot of emotional pain, that there are always lower bottoms to which we can sink. As my attitude continued to be negative and blaming, my situation worsened.

Only when I was willing to take responsibility for my life, stop blaming and look for what little good remained, was I able to begin to turn this situation around.

A negative attitude keeps us stuck by robbing us of the self discipline we need to improve our conditions. If you take a "what's the use" approach to your circumstances, they will only get worse.

It's imperative that you turn a negative attitude around and learn to become a positive person. Use the principles, techniques and ideas in this book to assist you.

Gratitude

The fastest and easiest way I know to change from a negative to a positive attitude is to develop an attitude of gratitude. You may even want to keep a gratitude journal, a place where you can build a list of the things you are grateful for in your life.

It's impossible to have gratitude and be in self pity at the same time, and most negative attitudes are rooted in self pitying, "poor me" self talk. You can quickly change a negative attitude to a positive one by becoming grateful.

The simplest way I know to do this is to ask a question like, "What am I grateful for today?" Then, write down whatever comes to mind. It may be all of the blessings you have like good health, a clear mind, a loving family, satisfying work, a comfortable home, friends, pets and so on.

Make a daily habit of counting your blessings and list what you are grateful for in your life. Doing this first thing in the morning will help you feel better immediately and begin your day on a positive note.

On days when you are feeling down, take out your "gratitude journal" and reread it. Doing this simple exercise will make you feel better almost immediately.

Action

While we will discuss action in more detail later in this book, I wanted to touch on it here because this one simple distinction can have a major impact in your life.

Too many of us spend our lives fence sitting, trying to decide what to do in any given situation. One of the chief characteristics of virtually all highly successful people is that they make decisions quickly and rarely, if ever, change them.

Unsuccessful people, on the other hand, take a long time deciding what to do and change their minds at the drop of a hat.

When you are faced with making a decision, after carefully weighing the facts, make your choice and act on it immediately. In almost any situation, doing something is usually better than sitting, waiting for something to happen.

There have been times in my business life when I didn't know what to do next. Times when I was scared and confused. If you are in your own business, you can probably identify with this situation. What I found was that, if I just acted — went out and saw people, made a call, wrote a letter — the situation would begin to change for the better. Taking action puts us in what is known as the "path of probability." You're a lot better off doing something than just sitting around waiting for something to happen.

Our tendency, especially in stressful situations, is to become like the ostrich and put our heads in the sand, or under the blankets as the case may be. Gripped by fear we do nothing. The problem is that doing nothing produces the same result — nothing!

Taking action will always produce a result. If you are un–sure about what to do, especially in your business, do something. Do whatever comes to mind first. As you begin taking action, keep going and the right action will become clear to you.

It has been said "Trust in the Divine, apply what you know, and the next step will be given."

EXERCISE — IMMEDIATE ACTION

Write in your journal any situations or challenges you are facing. Next to each one, write one simple action you can take immediately to help resolve it.

Once you've accepted your situation, shifted your attitude and decided to act, the next step on your way to creating the life of your dreams is *believing*. Believing you can do something about your situation.

Whatever it is you want to change it's critical for you to develop the belief that you can change it. If you feel stuck and think you are a victim of circumstances, you first need to change your belief to one of possibility and power.

One of the reasons you identified the changes you want to make, accepted and "owned" everything in your life is, that by doing so, you gain the power to change them.

CHAPTER 2 – BELIEFS

"What would you attempt to do if
you knew you could not fail?"

DR. ROBERT SCHULLER

Henry Ford said "Whether you believe you can, or you believe you can't, you're right." The quality of your life, your actions and your accomplishments, are all determined by your beliefs. This is a powerful and challenging statement; however, it's one that you'll realize is true once you have examined the concept of beliefs.

Why elephants don't run

A number of years ago, I had the rather unique experience of visiting backstage in Madison Square Garden, in New York, during the Ringling Brothers Barnum & Bailey Circus. To say the least, it was a fascinating experience. I was able to walk around looking at the lions, tigers, giraffes and all the other circus animals. As I was passing the elephants, I suddenly stopped, confused by the fact that these huge creatures were being held by only a small rope tied to their front leg. No chains, no cages. It was obvious that the elephants could, at any time, break away from their bonds but for some reason, they did not. I saw a trainer near by and asked why these beautiful, magnificent animals just stood there and made no attempt to get away.

"Well," he said, "when they are very young and much smaller we use the same size rope to tie them and, at that age, it's enough to hold them. As they grow up, they are conditioned to believe they cannot break away. They believe the rope can still hold them, so they never try to break free."

I was amazed. These animals could at any time break free from their bonds but because they believed they couldn't, they were stuck right where they were.

Like the elephants, how many of *us* go through life hanging onto a belief that we cannot do something, simply because we failed at it once before? How many of *us* are being held back by old, outdated beliefs that no longer serve us? How many of *us* have avoided trying something new because of a limiting belief? Worse, how many of *us* are being held back by someone else's limiting beliefs?

Beliefs aren't facts

Just because someone believes something cannot be done (even a large group of people) does not make it true. Be careful not to confuse beliefs with facts. People used to believe you couldn't run a mile in less than four minutes until a man named Roger Banister did it and proved them wrong. Today, high school students break the four–minute mile. At one time, everyone believed the world was flat. Did that make it so? Of course not. But until a young man named Christopher Columbus came along, it was a widely held belief. Until Louis Pasteur, most of society didn't believe in germs and bacteria, largely because they couldn't see them.

One word of caution here, be careful of global beliefs and social proof. That's when enough people agree on something, that it's assumed to be a fact. People told Wilbur and Orville Wright that they were crazy. Man was not meant to fly. Right! And automobiles will never replace the horse-drawn carriage.

At this point you may be asking, "What does all this have to do with me and my life-long success?" Well, it has everything to do with you and your life-long success.

The effort that you expend and the results that you achieve are directly related to your beliefs. In Napoleon Hill's historic words, "Whatever you can conceive and believe, you can achieve."

Beware of limiting beliefs

If you are in your own business and you hold a limiting belief that you aren't very good in sales, (this is a common belief held by many non-sales professionals) the effort you expend won't tap your true potential, and you will produce a less than desirable result.

Let's look at this idea more closely. Most people would agree that human potential is essentially unlimited. Then why don't we see this in our own lives? The problem and the reason most people aren't demonstrating their limitless potential is that their actions are tempered by their limiting beliefs. Because of a limiting belief, we tap only a small portion of our potential, which in turn, causes us to take limited action resulting in a limited outcome. *Becoming self perpetuating limitations*

In the case of your sales efforts, if you hold the belief that you aren't a good sales person, your effort will be half-hearted. You may only make a few sales calls and your results will be poor. We compound the problem by using the poor result as reinforcement for our limiting belief. We say something like "See, I told you I can't sell this stuff."

On the other hand, if you develop a belief that says, "I'm a great sales person," you will tap more of your potential, use more of your inherent creativity and take more action. The belief coupled with action will produce a greater result. Successful people assume success to be the natural outcome of their efforts.

Wayne Dyer wrote a book entitled *Transformation, You'll See It When You Believe It.* Dyer's simple yet powerful philosophy is that when you begin to believe in your success, you'll see the result in your life. When you begin to believe in your ability to reach your goals, you'll see your beliefs manifest on a physical plane.

Challenging your beliefs

Particularly in starting or running a business, we are cautioned not to take risks, usually by well–intentioned friends and family. How many of us have heard, "You can't do that!" These are the dream stealers who, due to their own limiting beliefs, will attempt to discourage you from living your dreams. You must ignore them at all cost! I'm not suggesting that you should not seek advice from qualified individuals and mentors, but that you avoid like the plague being swayed by the limiting beliefs of others, especially people who aren't in their own business.

Challenge your own limiting beliefs by questioning them. If you begin to question a belief, you automatically weaken it. The more you question your limiting beliefs, the more they are weakened. It's like kicking the legs out from under a stool. Once you weaken one leg, the stool loses its balance and falls.

We all sell

Think back to a time when you "sold" someone on yourself. We are selling all the time. You have to sell your ideas to your spouse, your children, your employees — even your banker. Maybe, as a child, you sold Girl Scout cookies or magazine subscriptions to raise money for your school team. Even though it was for your school, that was selling too!

Once you realize you are, in fact, a capable salesperson, you have weakened that old belief and began to replace it with a new, empowering one. Look for references to support the new beliefs you want to cultivate. As in the example of the stool, you want to reinforce your beliefs by adding more and more "legs" to them. Find people who have accomplished what you want to accomplish, discover what they did and model their behavior. Remember back to times in your past when you were successful and use that experience to propel yourself forward. If your challenge is in sales, read sales books and listen to tapes or attend sales seminars. Strengthen your sales "legs" so that you strengthen your *belief.* Whatever you do, don't be undermined by limiting beliefs.

Act as if

There is a technique called *fake it until you make it* that works well. I'm not suggesting you misrepresent yourself. I'm only suggesting that you begin to see yourself succeeding. Visualize your successes. See yourself vividly in your minds eye making the sale and reaching your goals. Affirm, over and over, that you are succeeding. Write your affirmations daily. Of course, make sure you take the appropriate action. As it says in the Bible, "Faith without works is dead."

Mental conditioning

Remember that your subconscious mind does not know the difference between real and imaginary. Before you go on a sales call, take a moment and mentally rehearse the scene, just like actors and athletes do. Tell yourself, "I'm a great salesperson." Do this over and over, especially just before a sales call. See the sale being made. See and feel the success. You will be pleasantly amazed at the result. Don't take my word for it. Give it a try. You have nothing to lose and everything to gain.

Ed and the car

An amusing example of this idea is the story told to me by my friend Ed. Ed had just finished attending a sales training program where he was taught that, just before calling on a prospective customer, in order to put himself in a peak mental and physical state, he should run around his car a few times.

Ed, anxious to use what he had learned, did this just before going in to see a new prospect at a major account. The meeting went well. The man liked Ed and his presentation and agreed to hire Ed's company.

The man was escorting Ed out of the building when he turned to Ed and said, "Ed, I have one question. I really like you and enjoyed your presentation and I feel good about working with your company but I was wondering, why were you running around your car in the parking lot?

It turns out, the man's office window looked out exactly on the spot where Ed had parked his car. His important prospect had watched him making a fool of himself running around his car! Blushing, Ed told the man the story. They both had a good laugh and Ed gained a new friend and customer.

Don't be an elephant

It has been said throughout history that whatever you believe with conviction, you can achieve. Don't be like the poor elephant and go through your life stuck because of a limiting belief you developed years ago. Take charge of your life and live it to the fullest. You deserve the best.

Where do beliefs come from?

Like the elephant, we have been conditioned by our beliefs. Many times, these aren't even our own. They originated from well-intentioned parents, teachers, and our peers while we were growing up.

I was given the belief that I couldn't draw. A grade school art teacher did not like a picture I had drawn and told me that I had no artistic talent. Unfortunately, I believed her most of my life and, consequently, have never enjoyed drawing or painting. A number of years ago I was able to disprove that with the help of a book titled *Drawing On The Artist Within,* by Betty Edwards. In it, she proves that anyone can learn to draw well. I was given the same negative belief about my singing ability. Perhaps one day I will change that as well. If at some future date you attend one of my seminars and see a band on stage, you'll know why! Fortunately for me, no one told me I couldn't write!

Dream crushers

Often, without even realizing it, our friends and families instilled destructive limiting beliefs in us. For example, most of us, when we discuss going into our own business, were met with things like "you can't do that", or "you'll never get ahead doing that" or "that's just a big scam, save your money." While these well-intentioned people were simply trying to prevent our getting hurt or failing, they were actually undermining our self–esteem and limiting our potential for success. That's why it's a good idea to be careful about who you share your dreams with, especially in the beginning. If you are starting a new business venture, beware of the dream crushers. There's another group of people you'll want to avoid, also. The not-so-well intentioned people who attempt to break our spirit because our success will force them to look at themselves and their own lack of accomplishment. Avoid all these naysayers!

Hang out with winners

What about your new empowering beliefs? How do you strengthen them? Again, you can find references to support your new beliefs. One of the reasons 12-step programs are successful is that the newcomer sees other people who have successfully changed their behavior and overcome their addiction.

If you want to change a limiting negative belief about the way you look, for example, seek out people who changed their physical appearance and find out what they did.

Changing of belief

Virtually all successful people are that way because they believe they will succeed in whatever they do. They expect to succeed. They assume success as the natural outcome of their efforts. They project, affirm, and visualize their success. The real danger with a limiting belief is that it will prevent you from even trying in the first place. It's only natural then to want to change those limiting beliefs that stand between you and the life of your dreams. The easiest and fastest way to change a belief is to challenge it. Our beliefs are held together by a supporting system of references. However, we can find references to support either side of a belief. We can find references to support the idea that politicians are crooks. There are enough of them in jail to support this belief. Or we can find references to support the opposite — that politicians are good and create positive change.

I can't because . . .

Whenever I give a workshop in a prison, I get the "I'll never get ahead because I'll always be an ex-convict" belief. I then tell the story of a local man who went from jail to a provisional job as a car washer at an auto dealership. He then was promoted to the service department. From there he went into sales and into sales management. And today, he is a vice-president with that organization. At that point, I ask who in the group knows of someone who got out of prison and was able to put their lives back together. Most of the hands in the group go up, as the men realize that they do have a chance. I explain to them that if they *believe* they can succeed, they will. I tell them my own story and how I rose from a lowly lifestyle because I *believed* I could.

Andy's a winner

A more amazing story is my friend Andy who, for most of his life, had the belief that his future was to be spent on a park bench drinking a bottle of wine. After all, he reasoned, that is all he had ever known. At one point he spent two years living in the Staten Island Ferry terminal in New York City. He thought this was a move up! Through the grace of God he got some help. He wound up getting a room at the Salvation Army, got into a treatment program, got off the booze and drugs, went to college, got a degree and the last time I saw him he had become a registered nurse and had a degree as a certified alcohol counselor. I've known countless people who have changed their situation in life by first changing their belief as to what was possible. Whatever your story, trust that you can change your circumstances. It begins with changing your limiting beliefs.

EXERCISE — CHANGING YOUR BELIEFS

In your journal, write three limiting beliefs that you now hold that you feel are preventing you from having what you want. They may be beliefs like, " I don't have enough money to start a business, or I grew up poor so I can't get ahead, or I can never lose weight because I'm big-boned." Whatever your limiting beliefs, choose three to five of them and write them down.

Next, write 3—5 *new* beliefs that you want to develop. What would you like to believe? What kinds of new beliefs would help you have the kind of life you want? What new beliefs would serve your needs now?

Fake it till you make it

Act as if you have already achieved your goals. Once you have completed the above exercise and identified your new empowering beliefs, you can begin to see yourself as being that person. You can act *as if* you have already become the person you want to be. For example, if you want to discard an old belief about being overweight, weak and unhealthy and develop a new empowering belief that you are fit, strong and healthy you can begin by acting the way a fit person would act. When faced with food choices, for example ask yourself, "What would the person that I want to become choose to eat?" If you want to be a successful entrepreneur, see yourself as already successful. Dress and look your best at all times. Act successful. Once again, in any situation ask "What would a successful person do in this situation?" "What would the person I want to become do in this situation?"

Trying on success

Another way to reinforce your new image of affluence is to do little things that will give you a glimpse of a more affluent lifestyle. Go to the best hotel in town, even to just sit in the lobby or to have a cup of coffee in the cafe. Feel the opulence. Get comfortable in the surroundings. They're all there for you to enjoy. You could begin browsing in more expensive stores to help you become accustomed to your impending success. If a new belief you want to cultivate is that of becoming a more loving parent and spouse, begin now by acting that way. Ask yourself, "How would a totally loving person handle this situation?" Do little things that will make you more loving. What would a loving person do for their family today? See yourself as being the new person you have decided to become. In a later chapter, we'll discuss visualization in more detail.

My old car

I remember some time ago having an old beat up car and wanting a new one. Having learned the principles I'm writing about here, I went to the dealership and obtained a picture of the car I wanted. I had all the information necessary. I knew the price, options, colors and every last detail of this automobile. I took the picture and hung it above my desk, where I would see it everyday. A short time later, I had the exact car in my driveway. Like all other successful people, I had achieved my goal first in my mind and then in reality.

Affirmations

Remember, your subconscious mind does not know the difference between the real and the imagined. I can prove that. If I were to ask if you would be willing to walk across a plank that is 20 feet long and 18 inches wide and had a $100 bill at the other end, and I put that plank on the ground in front of you and asked you to walk across it and pick up the $100, you would probably be more than happy to do that and you would have no problem with it. If, on the other hand, I were to take the same plank, the same $100, the same length, and just add one new dimension — just move that plank 50 stories into the air you would probably not want to do it. Logically, it's the same situation. It's the same plank. The only thing that changed was that your imagination got involved. Your imagination became part of the equation.

Logic vs. imagination

When logic and imagination come into conflict, imagination wins. You can harness this power and use it to your advantage. Invest some time each day thinking about what you want. Make mental pictures of what you want to become, using as much detail as you can. Be sure to include colors, sounds, scents and any other detail you can imagine.

Your subconscious mind does not know the difference between real and imagined. If you tell it over and over again that you are healthy and wealthy, it will believe you and direct you to the people, places and things that will make this true for you.

Pay attention

As you work with your affirmations, you will notice slight changes in your behavior. For example, you may notice that you are making healthier food choices or beginning to exercise. You may find yourself in a conversation about a business opportunity. These are the results of the work that you're doing internally. Be open to possibilities and trust that your Higher Power will guide you to your highest good. I suggest that you keep your affirmations simple, positive and in the present tense. In addition to "I approve of myself" you could write a simple affirmation that encompasses everything that you want to become. Something like "Every day in every way I'm becoming better and better and better." This was suggested by Claude Bristol in his wonderful work *The Magic of Believing*, one of the classics in self-help books written in 1948. I have used "I'm healthy, wealthy and successful" as my main affirmation. You can then devise other affirmations to address each area you are working on. Be sure to write them daily, if possible, 25 or 30 times or more and use mirror work. Reciting your affirmations in a mirror is one of the most powerful tools that you can ever use and will speed your progress immensely.

On the next page is a list of affirmations to help you get started. You can choose one or two of these or write your own:

I approve of myself

I'm a winner

I'm healthy, wealthy and successful

I'm fit and trim

I have total abundance in my life

I'm a wonderful, loving person

More money is flowing into my life

I deserve it

I deserve all good

I'm relaxed and at peace

Take a break, you deserve it

You have come a long way, my friend. Now that you have identified the areas in your life you want to change, learned to accept and own everything in your life, developed a more positive attitude, identified your limiting beliefs and developed new, empowering ones, you deserve a break. Take some time, a day or two, to let the material take hold in your life. Congratulate yourself. You are on your way to a more exciting, fulfilling and rewarding life.

CHAPTER 3 – DECISIONS & DREAMS

"It's a funny thing about life; if you refuse to accept anything but the best, you very often get it."

SOMERSET MAUGHAM

Everything you do — or for that matter, everything you don't do — begins with a decision. You decide whether or not to get out of bed in the morning. You decide what to wear. You decide whether to go to work or not, what to do when you get there, who to spend time with, and so on and so on. Often, these decisions are made unconsciously without much thought.

In the long run, the decisions we make or don't make affect the direction of our lives. You could decide to stay in bed and not go to work. However, if you did this on a regular basis, you wouldn't have a job to go to. Instead, you decide to go to work in order to earn the money to have what you want in your life.

In fact, everything in your life - your work, your relationships, your health - is a result of past decisions and choices.

If you want to make changes in your life (and who doesn't?), you must first *decide* to do so. If you want better health, decide right now to make a change. If you are in a dead–end job that you dread going to each day, decide right here and now to do something about it.

Decide to create the life you want and deserve. Today!

Change happens in an instant

All change is preceded by a decision. You can alter the direction of your life in an instant by deciding to change. Anyone who has ever succeeded in changing a habit of drinking, or eating, or smoking or even drugs has, at some point, come to a place where they made a decision to change. It was during that moment of decision that the change began. Granted, it may have taken years to get to that point, but the decision to change occurred in a flash.

My moment of truth

In the introduction, I wrote about myself and how my life sank to the depths of poverty before I reached what I consider my "bottom." This took years to occur. The conditions in my life worsened little by little over a period of 10 years. This is the way it happens to most people. Our lives slowly become worse without our even realizing how far down we've gone until, one day, we're at the bottom.

The change for me, however, occurred in a flash. I can remember the moment like it was yesterday, even though it was April, 1986. I was in a rented room in the south Bronx. My financial net worth was $3.85. My life was a disaster. I remember sitting on a worn out sofa, watching an old television with a coat hanger for an antenna, thinking, this is definitely not the Ritz Carlton. I clearly remember sitting there, my arms outstretched, looking up at the ceiling and saying to God, "I give up! Please either take me or help me. I can't go on like this." That moment, my life began to turn around. In that instant, my life changed. Something inside of me changed. I immediately felt a sense of hope and have never, from that moment on, had any craving for alcohol. The obsession to drink was lifted. This was the miracle in my life, and it happened in the blink of an eye. Of course, the rebuilding process took some time and will continue throughout my life. There is always room to grow.

You can decide right here, right now, that you are going to make the changes you outlined in the first chapter when you completed the exercise on page 18. If you haven't done this exercise, please go back now and complete it.

Decide now

In your journal, write a brief paragraph about what decisions you have made. Then date it and sign it. You might write something like this:

Today, I have decided I will take charge of my health and no longer eat foods that are unhealthy for my body. I will pay attention to my food intake and eliminate those foods that don't nourish my body. I have decided to begin my own part–time business in order to build a secure financial future. I will first investigate the opportunities available to me, choose one and, then pursue my new business to the best of my ability.

Sign your name to this. Once you have made the decision to change and to act, you are on your way to a better and more enjoyable life.

See it first

There is a wonderful story about the opening of Disney World in Orlando, Florida. A reporter who was interviewing Roy Disney, Walt Disney's brother exclaimed "It's too bad Walt did not live to see this." Roy quickly replied, "Walt saw it first. That's why you're seeing it now."

Walt Disney had a dream. He was one of the people who had not forgotten how to dream and to dream big. Walt knew that if he could imagine something, if he could dream it, he could make it a reality. The Disney Empire is a true testimony to the effects of a vivid imagination and the benefits of following your dreams.

The Bible tells us to become as little children. Walt Disney took that to heart and created an entertainment empire.

Children have no trouble imagining and dreaming. If you ask children what they want for Christmas, you'll most likely be given a long list. Ask an adult the same questions and you're likely to hear something like "I don't know" or "Oh, anything is fine, I don't need much." Why then do we as adults have such a hard time identifying what we want? Why do we believe it's our lot in life to simply accept whatever comes our way? Why are we afraid to dream and ask the Universe for what we want?

You are deserving

Are we supposed to settle? Are we so undeserving? Do you really believe our creator put all those wonderful things and experiences here on earth for someone else? If not, if you believe that all of the glory and wonderment is here for you too, then you owe it to yourself to relearn to dream.

What were you told?

"Stop dreaming! Be realistic! Get your head out of the clouds! Be thankful for what you have!"

Do any of the above statements sound familiar to you? If you are like most of us, you heard these over and over from family members, teachers and friends. While they may have been well-intentioned and meant to help us, they had the opposite affect.

Sure, you should be grateful for what you have. As a matter of fact, affirming your gratitude and counting your blessings is a powerful exercise and is great to do on a daily basis. However, dreaming of a bigger and better future doesn't mean you're not grateful for what you have now. It just means you want an even better future!

Norman Vincent Peals once said that if you want to have a big life, you need big dreams. If you want to have the kind of life you deserve, you need to begin dreaming again. Get back in touch with what you really want. What did you want as a child? What great dreams did you have that you may have forgotten? What do you want in your life now?

You have a dream

Everything in our world — every new labor saving device or invention, every breakthrough idea, every song ever sung, every book ever written, and every other accomplishment, large and small, began with a thought. Every great achievement was first a dream in the mind of the person who did it.

Martin Luther King had a dream, as did Gandhi, Mother Theresa, Walt Disney, Thomas Edison, Madame Curie, Henry Ford, Bill Gates, Ben & Jerry, Estee Lauder, Steve Jobs, George Lucas, Princess Diana, John F. Kennedy, Andrew Carnegie, Coco Chanel, and every great achiever since the beginning of time.

It works

The life I lead today began in my imagination several years ago. I envisioned living in a home in the country surrounded by woods with my loving wife and making a difference, doing work that I love. Today I'm living that dream. I receive letters daily from people who have been inspired to action by something they read in one of my books or articles. I get to spend my days writing and speaking to people all over the world and have the opportunity to share what I have learned with them.

Of course, I now have new dreams. The more I accomplish, the more I have, the bigger my dreams become. It's part of the natural expansion of the Universe.

My magic wand

Pretend for a moment that I have a magic wand. Remember, I asked you to become like a child again. I'm going to wave this magic wand over your head, and you will be granted whatever you desire. This is a magic wand, so there are no limits. You can have whatever your heart desires. You can do whatever you want to do. You can be whatever you want to be.

There are no limits

What do you want? If there were no limits (remember, this is a magic wand exercise) and you could manifest your dreams, all of them, what would that be? Would you want to climb the Matterhorn? Take a cruise to Alaska? Swim with dolphins? Sail the seas of the world? Have lunch atop the Eiffel Tower? Ride the Orient Express? Visit Disney World?

Do you want a new career? Your own business? Do you want to learn new skills? Play a musical instrument? Learn a foreign language? Get your degree? Learn a craft? Or perhaps, become a gourmet cook?

Would you like to become a better wife or husband? A more loving parent? A more spiritually connected person? Do you want more passion in your life? More excitement? More adventure?

Would a new car please you? What color? What make? How about a boat? Do you want a new house? A second home? New furniture? A stereo? A TV? A VCR? A camera? A computer? New carpeting? How about a new paint job?

Do you want to lose weight? Be healthier? Have a new hair style? Get braces? Be free of illness? Increase your energy?

Would you like more income? How much more? How about investments and savings? What would you do with an extra thousand dollars a month, or ten thousand dollars a month? Or even an extra *hundred thousand dollars a month?* Do you believe that's possible?

Clarity is a key

There are people who earn that kind of money — lots of them. The fact is that they are people just like you and me. The only difference is that they have become clear as to what they want in their lives and have taken action toward their goals. It's interesting to note that many highly successful people are that way because they're making a major contribution to society. They're the ones who are giving the most and, as it's written in the scriptures, are receiving the most as well.

What are your dreams? What do you want?

You can have whatever you want in this life. All of your dreams can come true. It's really a matter of deciding what you want and becoming willing to do something to have what you want.

EXERCISE — YOUR DREAMS

In your journal, write your dream sheet. Write down everything you want to do, to be, to have, and to share in your life. Remember, this is a magic wand exercise so don't worry about how you will accomplish these things. For now, all you want to do is gain some insight into what you really want. List everything you can think of, no matter how outrageous. Later we will zero in what's really important to you.

What do you want?

Don't let your logical mind get involved and start editing. Ignore the little voice that's saying "You can't do that" or "You can't have that, it's too expensive." Ignore it! Tell that little voice to be quiet just for now.

Logic and reason have their place, but it's not in a dreaming or brainstorming exercise. Most people never realize their potential because they let their reasoning mind talk them out of things before they even begin.

Here's what happens. You think to yourself, "I'd like a new luxury automobile." Before you even have a chance to settle in with the desire, your logical mind interrupts with something like, "Don't be foolish. Where will you get the money?" If you learn to ignore your reasoning mind for a while and just go with the dream, you may learn that there are many ways to accomplish your goal of a new car. You could, for example, get a job as a salesperson in an automobile dealership and have a demo car to use. You may even win a car. Or, you could make the necessary money and simply buy it. The point is to let your creative mind work on the desire before your logical mind dismisses it as frivolous.

Genius or lunatic?

Many years ago, Walt Disney had an idea for an amusement park. People told him he was crazy, that he couldn't charge admission simply to go into an amusement park; furthermore, the idea of an amusement park for adults was totally unheard of. Fortunately, a banker at Bank of America in California believed in Walt Disney and lent him the money to build Disneyland. Amazingly, the entire loan was paid back during the first year of operation. Wow!

One hundred and one wishes

Just write down everything that you can imagine having and becoming in your life. My friend Jack Canfield, co-author of the incredibly successful Chicken Soup for the Soul series, suggests in *The Alladin Factor*, another wonderful book he co–authored, that you write down 101 wishes. Take a couple of pages in your journal and write numbers from 1-101. I promise that once you have completed this exercise you'll have uncovered pretty much everything you could possibly want in your life.

Chapter 4 – Goals

"There are two ways to face the future. One way is with apprehension; the other is with anticipation."

Jim Rohn

When you go on vacation, do you stand patiently in an airport ticket line, step up to the counter, plop down your suitcase and say to the agent, "I want to go on a vacation, please sell me a ticket to somewhere"? Of course not. By the time you and your family leave for vacation, you have probably been planning it for months. You have decided and agreed upon where you want to go, developed your schedule, made travel and hotel arrangements, obtained brochures about the places you wanted to visit, picked out some attractions you want to see and special things you want to do there. You have most likely been talking about the trip — seeing yourselves there doing the things you want to do. Maybe you've been counting down the days until departure time, your excitement building until the "final moments." You and your family have probably "visited" there in your minds, time and time again. Finally, the day arrives and you head off on your long awaited, carefully planned, vividly imagined, constantly affirmed and reinforced family vacation.

"Wow, this is great," you say, as you actually experience the feeling you have imagined all along. It's even better than you imagined.

This is your life, not a dress rehearsal

If you were willing to put all this effort into planning your vacation, why then do you leave your life to chance? Why do you get up in the morning, shower, get dressed, walk out the door and just "wing it?" Surely your life deserves at least as much attention as your vacation!

Most people go through each day having no idea what they want or where they're going. It's a sad fact that most of us invest more time and energy into planning our vacations than planning our lives.

You, my friend, aren't one of these people. If you were, you wouldn't have picked up this book in the first place. No, you want more. The fact that you've read this far demonstrates that you want lifelong success.

In my opinion and in the opinion of many others, setting goals is the pivotal point on the path to success and happiness. Earl Nightingale, the famous motivational speaker and author, said it best when he defined success as, "The progressive achievement of a worthwhile goal." Zig Ziglar, one of the most significant success coaches of our time, reminds us that we "cannot return from a vacation we have not taken, and we cannot reach a goal we have not set." My feeling is that if you haven't defined what success means to you and have no measurable goals, how can you know if you are successful? If you don't know what success looks like, you won't recognize it when it shows up! It has been said that a person without a goal is like a ship without a rudder. I've always liked the analogy of a piece of Styrofoam bouncing around the ocean, moving in whatever direction the wind and waves take it. This is no way to live your life. Set goals!!

Purpose

Many years ago, a friend of mind defined purpose as "a reason to expend energy." Purpose gives us a reason to get out of bed in the morning. It keeps us going in the face of adversity. It gives us the inner strength we need to overcome any obstacle. If your purpose or goal is strong enough, you will find a way. Our goals help us to answer the question, "Why am I doing this"?

A while back, I had reached the point where I had to take some action toward improving my physical health and fitness. I was tired of the way I looked and felt. I had gained weight and had low energy most of the time. Sound familiar? I decided I had to change.

Following the steps I cover in this book and in my seminars, I set a goal to get in shape, to reach a specific weight by a specific date, and change some of my eating habits, eliminating certain foods from my diet. As part of my action plan (we will discuss this in the next chapter), I joined a health club. My goal was to work out between four and five times each week. My purpose was clear. I was on my way to victory!

One bitter, cold winter day, with the temperature below zero, my resolve was put to the test. In order to keep to my schedule and my commitment that particular week, I needed to go to the

gym at 6:00 a.m. on a day that was brutally cold. The only reason I was on a treadmill at 6:05 a.m. that freezing day is that I
had clearly defined my goal and had become committed to
achieving it. My purpose was clear.

Focus on results

Your purpose will get you through the tough (or cold) times.
An added benefit is the power you feel from having overcome
the tendency to lie in bed under the warm blankets.

Your purpose is the reason behind your goal. Your purpose is
why you want the goal in the first place.

In the 1960s, President John F. Kennedy set a national goal to
put a man on the moon before the end of the decade. This was
not because he wanted to learn if there really was green cheese
on the moon!

His purpose, and the reason he succeeded was to ensure that
the United States would remain a world power and not take a
back seat in the race into space. It's interesting to note that when
he set that particular goal, President Kennedy had no idea how
it would be reached. He did, however, have the other necessary
ingredients for success:

- The belief that it could be done

- The commitment to make it happen

- The willingness to take action, in this case, massive action.

Others were inspired by his goal and made it their own. In

1969, all the world watched their TVs as the first human being, an American named Neil Armstrong, walked proudly on the surface of the moon.

All successful people have clear goals.

Our home

Several years ago my wife, Georgia, and I were house hunting. Several factors were making it difficult to find a suitable house. Among them was the fact that our home was described as "hard to sell." One day, after returning from yet another unsuccessful day of house hunting, I watched my wife break into tears. I pulled the car over to the side of the road and tried to comfort her. I understood her frustration and shared her feelings. Something inside me clicked. I said, "Wait a minute. We're doing this all wrong," remembering my experiences and what I had learned. I said, "Let's do what I suggest in my writing. Instead of being concerned with selling our present house, let's focus on what we want, not on what we don't want and go from there. Let's set a goal, take the appropriate action, and leave the rest to God."

We decided that our anniversary, October 27th, would be our goal cut–off date. We wrote it down and went on about our business. Every few weeks, we would go and look at more houses, with no success.

Months passed and, frankly, I was beginning to wonder about the effectiveness of this goal–setting stuff myself. As our anniversary approached, we had planned to visit upstate New

York for a few days and then, on the day of our anniversary, go to Bucks County, Pennsylvania. Our New York trip was not what we wanted, so we called the bed & breakfast where we were scheduled to stay and asked to arrive a few days early. Keep in mind, we were "supposed" to be in upstate New York.

The day before our anniversary, we were driving from one location to another, looking at vacant lots. We had decided that if we couldn't locate the house we needed, we could always have it built. As we were riding to the next location, I glanced to my right and saw some huge homes being built. My first thought was, "They're too expensive," but Georgia suggested we stop anyway on the way back.

We did stop and spoke with the builder. It turned out they were within our price range. The hitch was there was only one lot that was suitable for us and we did not know if it would work. We needed to build a walk–out basement for Georgia's parents apartment.

This was one day before the target date to reach our goal! Our original plans had us a hundred miles away on that day but here we were. The arrangement worked out, and today, we live in this beautiful custom built home — a goal realized and truly a dream come true. No one will ever tell me goal–setting doesn't work. I know better!

Landmark study

You may have heard about the classic landmark study that was done at a major university in the 1950's. Researchers interviewed the graduating class and found that only 3% had written goals with plans for their achievement. They followed this group for twenty years. In 1974 or 1975 when they re–investigated the group, they found that in measurable areas, specifically financial success, the 3% who had written down their goals were worth more than the other 97% combined.

Goal setting — the mechanics

Here are some guidelines for writing your goals:

• They must be written in the present tense (I have, I am, I earn, Etc.). Your sub–conscious mind takes things literally. It does not respond to past or future tenses. Writing something like, "I will be having . . ." will instruct your sub–conscious mind to keep the goal out of reach — in the future.

• They must be stated in the positive. Writing "I will lose 20 pounds" won't work as well if it works at all. Your sub–conscious mind cannot work on the reverse of an idea. Negative commands like *Can't, won't, don't, lose, etc.* aren't interrupted by your sub–conscious mind.

For example, if I say to you, "Don't think of a pink elephant" what happens? If I say, "Think of anything you want but don't think of a pink elephant," you immediately think of a pink elephant, right? It's the same with your goals. Keep them in the positive. Rather than "I will lose 20 pounds," you could write, "On or before (date), I'm at my ideal weight of 120 pounds."

• When dealing with goals that can be measured (weight, finance, etc.), be as specific as possible and have a target date.

For example, a goal of "more money" is not like to produce much of a result; it's too vague. A better way to put it would be, "I'm in my own part–time business, earning an additional $1,000 per month on or before July 1."

One step at a time

It's a good idea to set goals for different time frames. Short, medium and long range goals all help to give our lives a sense of direction and work together to help us have the life of our dreams. An added benefit of shorter range goals is that the thrill of accomplishing them helps us to stay motivated. If all you had were long range goals it would be difficult to measure your progress and harder to keep yourself going in the face of set-backs. Personally, I like to set Short–term (3–6 months), One–year, Medium–term (3–5 years) and Long–term (10–20 year) goals.

That last one, the twenty year goal, I learned from Robert Schuller and it has been a real challenge, projecting my life out twenty years into the future. While circumstances will change, having a general idea of where I'm going makes my life more meaningful. Of course, I will modify these goals as I go along.

Chances are you will be there in 20 years. The big question is where will "there" be? What will your life be like in 20 years? What will you be doing? Who will you be? By dreaming it now and taking appropriate action, you can begin to create the life you will want to be living 20 years from now.

By working backwards, you can begin to take the necessary

actions today to bring you where you want to go. For example, if one of your long–range goals is financial independence, with enough passive income — that's income you don't have to labor for, like residual income, investment income, royalties, etc. — for the rest of your life you will see that one of your short–term goals needs to be beginning an investment program, going into your own business or doing something that will enable that to take place.

Beware of self sabotage

Some people avoid writing and setting goals because they're afraid they won't reach them. So what! If you don't set goals you surely won't reach them because you won't have them in the first place.

There are ways to change this self defeating thinking. First, make sure your goals are within reach for the time period you set. A goal of being 20 pounds lighter by next Thursday is not likely to work unless you are giving birth to a baby! Give yourself sufficient time to accomplish the goal. Goals should, however, be a stretch for you. Don't make them too easy. You want to challenge yourself and "push the envelope" to stretch out of your comfort zone.

Secondly, if you miss a goal, move the date or rewrite the goal. They are written in your journal, not carved in stone!

You can't fail

By setting goals, writing them down and taking action, you

will succeed. You are already ahead of 97% of the population. Just by having set your goals your likelihood of succeeding increases greatly.

Even if you don't fully reach your goal, you will have made more progress and accomplished more than if you had not set goals in the first place.

This past year, I set a goal to read two books each month. My plan was to read each day and by the end of the year to have read 24 books. Well, things changed. My circumstances changed and my schedule became heavier. There were many days when I shortened my reading time.

Interestingly enough, because I had set a goal, I ended the year having read 19 books. Though I missed my original target goal, I'm far better off than if I had not set it in the first place. By the way, I did not factor in the dozens of audio cassettes I listened to throughout the year. This year, my goal will include audio books too, and the goal will be higher.

It has been said that:

If you reach for the moon and miss, you still have the stars.

If you set a goal to increase your income by $3,000 a month and only succeed in increasing it by $2,000, have you failed? Will you give the money back? Not likely. You are still way ahead of where you would be if you had not set the goal in the first place.

If you take only one thing from this book, let it be goal setting. Having written goals and plans for their achievement is one of the most powerful ideas you will ever use. Goals are magical. They have a way of coming true — sometimes in the strangest ways, but they do come true.

EXERCISE — GOAL SETTING

Find a comfortable place where you won't be disturbed for a while. Allow sufficient time to complete this exercise. It may be one of the most important things you ever do. In your journal, set aside several pages for writing your goals. Go back to the exercise in the first chapter and look at the different areas of your life. Be sure to set goals in all these areas.

Go to the dream sheet exercise you completed earlier. This is where you wrote all your dreams and aspirations. Using this list as a guide, pick the ones that are most important to you. You may want to begin with the short–term and one–year goals for now and work up to the longer range ones.

In your journal, write one or two short–term goals from each category on a page or two. Be sure to leave space between them. Under each goal, write a short sentence about why you want this goal. What will having it mean to you? What will you get by reaching it? Go back to the exercise on commitment and use that as a guide. The more reasons you have for wanting the goal, the more likely you will do what is necessary to reach it. Do this for each of your short–term and one–year goals. Later you can come back and complete this for longer term goals.

CHAPTER 5 – ENERGY & ENTHUSIASM

"Nobody grows old merely by living a number of years. We grow old by deserting our ideals. Years may wrinkle the skin, but to give up enthusiasm wrinkles the soul."

SAMUEL ULLMAN

How many of you come home from work, eat dinner and plop down on the couch in front of the TV because you're too tired to do anything else? Maybe you even eat in front of the TV. Unlike the Energizer Bunny, do your batteries run down around 3 o'clock in the afternoon? Are you just too beat to do any more?

To have an exciting and productive life, to live your dreams and reach your goals, you will need abundant amounts of energy. It takes energy and physical health to enjoy life to the fullest. Unfortunately, most of our society lacks both the physical health and the stores of energy required to live fully. Too many of us, even children, lack the physical capacity to live the kind of life we want and deserve. Americans in particular are in such poor health and so unfit it has become a global embarrassment.

The good news is that it's never too late to change your physical condition. While you may have physical challenges that you cannot do anything about, there's always room for improvement in your overall condition. If you want proof of this, all you have to do is watch the Special Olympics and see how people with serious perceived physical challenges have persevered regardless of their condition. Beginning from where you are, decide now to take better care of your physical health.

You are what you eat

While there have been enough books written about what to eat and what not to eat to fill a good size bookstore, I would like to offer one simple suggestion on this subject. Whether you prefer to follow a diet of vegetarian, herbivore, fruitarian, or as one person put it "an omnivore" (that's someone who eats whatever they want), there is a simple rule of thumb that will help you maintain a healthier food program.

Simply obtain 70-80% of your food from fruits and vegetables. If you do this, you will automatically become healthier. Of course, you need to apply common sense as well.

In their series of *Fit for Life* books, Harvey and Marilyn Diamond explain this concept by pointing out that we are made up of 70-80% water. For that matter, our entire planet is 70-80% water. So it stands to reason that eating water–rich foods such as fruits and vegetables is good for us. One easy way to reach this level of water–rich foods is to eat a large, fresh salad with each meal.

Moderation in all things

Another key is moderation. A doctor once suggested to me that if I really wanted to have ice cream, go ahead, only have it once a week, not every night. This was something I was able to do without too much trouble.

An apple a day

Another great suggestion I learned from the noted speaker and trainer, Brian Tracy. He suggests eating an apple or two in the morning instead of a big breakfast. I know there is a lot of controversy about breakfast being an important meal, but modern research doesn't support that. Personally, I find an apple or two works great. There is enough sugar to give my brain the nourishment it needs (glucose), and apples are low in fat. Over the course of a few years, I have found this to work well as long as I eat a light lunch early in the day. A fringe benefit is that apples are easy to eat on the run, a practice that many of us have adopted.

An apple a day helps us to remain healthy because, among other things, apples contain large quantities of malic acid, a substance which helps fight bacteria and aids digestion. The old adage that "An apple a day keeps the doctor away" did not just become a cliche for no reason. Of course I occasionally have an egg breakfast complete with muffins or bagel because life is meant to be enjoyed, right?

If you're really serious about having better health, it's worthwhile to learn about nutrition. Your health is critical and it warrants your seeking professional advice to assist you in living the healthiest life you can. By all means, have regular checkups at least once a year with a qualified medical professional.

Physical exercise

No discussion about energy would be complete without

bringing up exercise. You've heard the expression, "Use it or lose it!" A simple exercise program, one that will keep your body reasonably fit and your heart working well, does not take a lot of time and can be enjoyable. The key is to find an activity or several activities you enjoy and develop a regular routine. One of the best and simplest overall fitness programs is simply to take a walk for 30-40 minutes several times a week. It costs nothing and does not require special equipment. You may even want to consider a personal trainer to help you design a program that's right for you. One word of caution - begin any exercise routine slowly, and, to prevent injury, never force your body. Of course, see your medical professional before beginning any exercise program.

Learn to breathe

When was the last time you took a really deep breath? If you are like most people, breathing is something you take for granted. We assume we're breathing correctly but that's not necessarily true. Most people have a very shallow breathing pattern, and this can add to our everyday stress. When we get anxious, we tend to take short, rapid breaths.

One way to relax under pressure is to purposely slow your breathing and take long, deep breaths. Some time ago, a friend taught me a breathing technique which has been very useful for reducing my stress. It's something I can use at any time during the day if I feel a bit tense.

The technique itself is pretty simple. All you need do is take slow, steady breaths. Inhale to a count of five and exhale slowly, to the same count. Do this five or ten times. If you're going to try this, please remember not to strain at any time and to stop if you feel dizzy or light–headed.

Be still and know

A lot has been written about the benefits of quiet time. It reduces stress, speeds healing, lowers your heart rate and can help you stay centered. All you really need to do is sit quietly for twenty minutes or so each day. Simply focus your attention on your breathing and quietly follow your breath as it enters and leaves your body. If your mind wanders and begins to focus on your chores or worries, gently bring it back and watch your breathing. Do this in a quiet place where you won't be interrupted.

Set your priorities

Your physical and mental health and well being are at the center of your life. You can't feel successful if you are physically tired or stressed out. Make your health a #1 priority. Many people sabotage themselves because they try to squeeze meditation and exercise into their busy schedules. If you want to succeed, rearrange your lifestyle to accommodate your wellness routines. Make it the most important thing on your "to do" list. Whatever your present physical condition, you can make small daily improvements and over time, look, feel and be significantly healthier and happier. Go for it. You deserve it.

Enthusiasm & Excitement

Get excited about life. As the title of this book suggests, This is your life; it's not a dress rehearsal! Be enthusiastic.

I remember sitting in an office one day waiting for an appointment when a secretary covered her typewriter and with a big sigh proclaimed, "Well I made it through another day." I thought to myself "how sad." It was almost as if she was just checking off the days one by one until her life was over. Is this any way to live? I think not. I know you don't want to live life like this or you wouldn't be reading this book. Life is meant to be enjoyed. Life is exciting. If you don't believe me, watch a small child.

Through the eyes of a child

One sunny summer afternoon I had the wonderful experience of taking a walk with a friend's three year old. I had not been around a small child for quite some time and had forgotten how much children enjoy life. There is no such thing as ordinary or routine for a three or four year old. They see the wonderment in all of life. I remember at one point we stopped to watch an insect cross the sidewalk. On another occasion we stopped to examine the cracks in the sidewalk. Nothing escaped this little child. It was all exciting and interesting.

Be here, now

Children are more enthusiastic because they live in the present moment. They aren't beating themselves up about mistakes they made yesterday, nor are they worried about tomorrow. They are right here, right now.

The more we remind ourselves about *being here — now*, the happier and more successful we will be.

Learn to be in the present moment. Each day, when I awaken, I take a few moments and ask God to guide me to take the right action for today. I ask, "How can I make the most of this precious day?" The more I stay centered in the now, the better I feel and the more I accomplish.

The times when I "spin my wheels" are those times when I lapse into trying to change something beyond my control, like the past or fretting about some future event. Live today. I once read a little poem that helps me to remember this:

> *Yesterday is history*
> *Tomorrow is a mystery*
> *Today is a gift*
> *That's why it's called the present!*

Stop and smell the roses

How much of the joy and beauty of life do you stop and notice each day? Do you see the majestic sunrise as the light radiates across the early morning sky? Do you take in the freshness of the early morning air and bask, even if just for a moment, in the beauty of a newborn day? Or are you too busy getting ready for work? Do you, as they say, take time to stop and smell the roses?

There has never been a person who, on their death bed, said they wished they had spent more time at the office. Take the time to enjoy your life. Make a practice of noticing the small, everyday sights and sounds in your world.

What about your work? Are you excited and enthusiastic about what you do? Or are you like the secretary, just trying to make it through the day?

Too many people in our society, as Henry David Thoreau said, are "leading lives of quiet desperation."

Wake up

Get excited about your life. When someone asks you how you are, rather than simply saying okay or fine, try saying great! Say it with enthusiasm and you will be amazed at how often you will begin to feel better as a result of doing this.

Move and walk with enthusiasm. Put some bounce in your step and stand tall. This is your life. Live it with zest!

Try jumping out of bed in the morning with expectancy for the coming day instead of dragging yourself up complaining. Look to each day as the gift that it is. Norman Vincent Peal suggested a passage from the Bible that can help you awaken feeling expectant and joyful: *This is the day which the lord has made. We will rejoice and be glad in it.* Reciting this passage first thing after awakening helps me start the day on a positive note.

Questions

If you read my first book, *Handbook to a Happier Life* you may remember the section about morning questions. These are questions you develop to help put you in a positive frame of mind. Ask questions like: What am I excited about today? What am I looking forward to today? What am I grateful for? What makes me happy? Find something in your work to excite you. Find something you are looking forward to experiencing this day and focus on that for a few minutes before you arise.

Doing this will help put you in a positive, expectant and enthusiastic state of mind. Remember, our questions determine what we focus on, and our focus determines the quality of our experiences.

If you are walking down the street in a large American city, you can choose to focus on the beauty of the tall buildings or you can choose to focus on the garbage and litter. Your choice will greatly affect your experience of that city.

Chapter 6 – Fear & Faith

"You may be deceived if you trust too much, but you will live in torment if you do not trust enough"

Dr. Frank Crane

If you are to have the kind of life you want and deserve, you must learn to overcome your fears. Fear is the single biggest destroyer of dreams and has prevented more people from having what they want than any other factor. It prevents you from taking the actions necessary for your success and can keep you stuck right where you are.

Operating from a position of fear we tense up, reducing the blood flow to our brain, which further complicates the situation. Now, not only are we in a fearful state, our thinking and ability to solve our problem is greatly hindered. I cannot emphasize enough how important it is to learn to break through, go around, go over or under or whatever it takes to move past fear and into action.

One way to do this is to develop a strong unshakable faith in God and know, that if we will simply do our part, everything will work out. Notice I said "do our part." Because there are clearly actions we can take in any situation and we must be willing to take them. I've always liked the statement that God moves mountains, but remember to bring a shovel.

Natural fears

It's interesting to note that we are born with only two fears.

The fear of loud noises and the fear of falling. All of the others are learned. We often tell children not to do certain things for fear they could be hurt. Sometimes this is good. Like in the case of teaching a child not to venture out into traffic. However, sometimes, with the best of intentions, we become overly protective and can actually stifle the child's natural curiosity. As we grow from children into adults, we carry our fears with us and can develop a habit of not trying new things, or of not deviating from the status quo. As adults, our reluctance to try new things is actually our fear of failure.

Risk

If you never risk, you cannot fail. Unfortunately, you cannot succeed either. In order to become the person you are capable of becoming, there will be times when you will need to take small, calculated risks. To live the kind of life you deserve, you will need to face your fears and take action to overcome them.

The three faces of fear

Fears tend to fall into one of three categories. The fear of failure, the fear of being hurt and the fear of not being perfect. I realize the last one, the fear of not being perfect, may sound a bit strange, but many times we won't attempt something because we are holding on to a belief that we must be perfect in everything we do. We have been conditioned to be overly critical of ourselves and to expect unrealistic performance and results when, in fact, we are as the Billy Joel song so aptly points out, only human.

How many of you don't participate in an activity because you feel you are "not good enough?" Do you avoid dancing, singing, playing a sport or public speaking simply because you feel a need to be perfect before you even attempt it?

Do what you fear

The irony is that the way people become great at these activities is by doing them. The easiest way to overcome the fear of not being perfect is by allowing yourself to be less than perfect. Give yourself permission to feel uncomfortable with an activity until you have done it long enough to have acquired the skills needed to do it well. Don't let your perfectionism prevent you from partaking in and enjoying the many activities life has to offer. Do you really believe that everything Van Gogh, Dali or DaVinci painted was brilliant? It's unlikely. I'm sure if you look at their early attempts you will see less than great art.

Did Billy Joel or Elton John jump out of their cribs and start writing hit songs? Their beginning efforts were probably not worth recording. As a matter of fact, Billy Joel once felt so much a failure that he considered taking his own life. Fortunately, he sought help and has gone on to become one of the most successful song writers of our time. When you were a child, did you just get up one day and start walking? I doubt it. You most likely crawled first, then began a ritual of standing, stumbling and falling. After a period of trial and error you finally succeeded. The fact that you can walk today is only because you were willing to be "less than perfect" in your early attempts. So the next time the music starts playing, come out dancing.

> *Remember that when you do that which*
> *you fear, the death of fear is certain.*

Fear of failure

In *Handbook to a Happier Life* I wrote, "There is no such thing as failure. Every action produces a result." Think about it. Whatever you are attempting to do, if you take an action, you will produce a result. It may not be the result you were looking for, but it will be a result nonetheless.

You cannot fail

Too many of us will let our fear of "failure" prevent us from taking any action at all. This is especially true for people who are considering going into their own business. The question, "What if I fail?" pops up immediately. Somehow we convince ourselves we won't succeed even before we begin. This is, however, understandable because most of us have been conditioned to think like this.

Most, if not all, successful entrepreneurs have had setbacks along the way. The difference is that they view them as setbacks, while unsuccessful people consider the same outcomes as failures and give up before they even have a chance to succeed.

If you reframe so called "failure" and see it for what it really is — a temporary setback or learning experience — you will increase your chances of success.

Great failures

When Thomas Edison was asked, after finally succeeding in inventing the electric light after about 10,000 attempts, what it was like to fail all those times he replied, "I did not fail. I simply discovered thousands of ways that wouldn't produce electric light." On another occasion, he quipped that he succeeded because he had exhausted all of the ways that wouldn't work.

Sometimes the result you produce by overcoming your fear of failure can be even more than you expected. Christopher Columbus set out to find a shortcut to India only to discover a New World. Was he a failure?

Three step solution

To break through your fear of failure, take action, gauge the result and modify your action until you achieve the result you want.

An airplane flying from San Francisco to Maui is off course about 90 percent of the time. Comforting, isn't it? In reality it's not a problem since the plane's computer is constantly making minor corrections in the flight path until the plane lands safely in Hawaii. Being off track is part of the process and is quite natural.

You can do the same. By gauging the results of your actions, eliminating what is not working and emphasizing what works, you can produce the results you're looking for. This applies as much to health and fitness or relationships as it does to your venturing into your own business.

The fear of being hurt

Your fear of being hurt, bumped, bruised, embarrassed, laughed at or just having your ego dented is another fear that you'll need to overcome if you want to become all you are capable of becoming.

You'll never know your true potential or live your life to the fullest if you're not willing to risk some small hurts, real or imagined. I'm *not* suggesting that you put yourself in danger of being physically harmed or that you gamble everything you have and risk financial ruin.

I'm referring to those "little" hurts — usually to our egos — that come from stepping out of our comfort zone and taking risks. Here's an examples from my own experience as an author. When I was writing my first book, I was in a very comfortable, non-threatening space called *writing a book*. I could tell people, "I'm writing a book." It was safe and secure. I couldn't fail or be rejected as long as I remained in the writing stage.

Unfortunately, unless I was willing to risk rejection, I would be the only person who would ever read it!

In order to experience all of the wonderful feelings and victories that come from being a *successful* author, I had to step out of my comfort zone, publish the book, and then sell it.

As long as I was in the "writing" stage, I was very safe. However, in order to succeed, I had to risk. Fortunately for me, *Handbook to a Happier Life* has been a huge success, and I have experienced that wonderful feeling that comes from knowing that people are using something I wrote to make positive changes in their own lives.

Breaking through fear

Feel your fear and move on. To simplify the process, let me suggest the following:

1. Face your fears. You cannot deny your fear. If you have a fear of calling people you don't know, a definite disadvantage in your own business, you need to acknowledge it.

2. Analyze the fear.

What fear is stopping you from having what you want?

What is the worst that can happen if you go for it?

How likely is that to happen?

Can you live with it if it did?

3. Visualize success. See your action producing a successful outcome.

4. Break the pattern. Do something. Get up and move around the room. Chant, jump up and down, do something physical for a few minutes to get your energy up.

5. Go for it. Once you are feeling more powerful, pick up the phone and start dialing. Once you're in the process, the fear will dissipate. While you may never learn to enjoy calling total strangers on the telephone (few people do), you will have interrupted the fear long enough to get past it.

You can't lose what you don't have

One last thought on the subject of fear. Many times people will avoid doing something for fear they won't succeed when, in reality, if they *did not succeed,* they would be no worse off than they are.

Let me explain. You're at a party and, across the room, you see that "perfect" person. You want to go over and ask them to dance but hesitate because you're afraid they'll say no. Think about this for a moment. If you were to go over and ask the person to dance and they said no, where would you be? You'd be exactly where you are — not dancing! You wouldn't have lost anything. You can't lose what you don't have.

In business, when you let your fears prevent you from asking for an order, the situation is the same. If I'm not your customer now and you ask me for an order and I say no, I'm still not your customer. You haven't given up anything other than a slight bump to your ego, which you'll get over.

FAITH

"If you believe, you will receive whatever you ask for in prayer "

MATTHEW 21:22

The best way to overcome fear is to develop a strong, unshakable faith. There is a wonderful little story that goes:

Fear knocked on the door. When faith answered, there was no one there.

Develop a strong faith

Faith is that sense of knowing, even though you cannot yet see the result, that everything will work out for your own highest good. As the above quote from the Bible says "If you have faith, everything you ask for in prayer you will receive." It does not say some of what you ask for. It does not say, "Up to a certain level you will receive," It says "Everything."

Faith is the inner "knowing" that you will achieve your desired result in any undertaking. It's believing even though you have no proof. It's trusting and "becoming as a child" in your trust.

Trusting your inner guidance

There have been many times in my past when I was stuck and didn't know what to do next. At these times perhaps, we all experience a test of our faith.

When faced with these challenges, I focus on my goal, take action and *"let go and let God."* This is very similar to what the Bible says, that "faith without works is dead." It seems clear to me that the message is have faith, take action and trust that it will all work out.

Sometimes we may feel we don't have enough faith or any at all for that matter. That is nonsense. Think about all the acts of faith you perform each day. In it's simplest form, you demonstrate faith each time you exhale. You don't worry about where your next breath will come from, do you? Yet, we worry about where the rent money or car payment will come from.

I have been in that situation more times than I'd like to remember, and, looking back, I now realize that whenever things didn't work out, it was because I wasn't taking action on my faith.

When I became willing to act and did what I intuitively felt was the right action, everything worked out fine.

We don't fret that the sun will rise tomorrow. We have the trust and faith that it will. We drive our automobiles down two-lane roads at 60 miles per hour and trust that the other cars will remain on their side of the dividing line. We don't question. We just have faith that it will all work out, and it usually does. Why then do you worry needlessly about the rest of your life?

Trust in God

If you are doing what you feel in your heart is right, and you are taking care of your part in the play (as Shakespeare said), then simply trust in God and know that all is well.

What I have found to be fascinating is that what we ask for becomes manifest because of our faith that it will.

If you set out to achieve a result, whether it's in health, business, relationships, finance, education or your spiritual life, and you know deep in your heart that something will occur and you hold to that unshakable faith, it must, as is promised in the Bible, come to pass.

Your success is directly proportional to your faith in your ability to succeed

CHAPTER 7 – CHOICES & COMMITMENT

"Our grand business in life is not to see what lies
dimly at a distance, but to do what
lies clearly at hand."

THOMAS CARLYE

As we walk down the pathway of our lives, we are constantly making choices — good and not so good — that affect where
we are going. As Yogi Berra, the great baseball star and
American Philosopher once said to the graduating class at
Harvard, "As you go through life you will come to a fork in the
road. Take it." I think people like Yogi, while he has had little
formal education, are profound in their observations of life. We
make choices all day long. What to wear, where to go, what to
eat, who to be with, and on and on. Many of these we make
unconsciously, operating more out of habit than anything else.

How many times have you been in a restaurant at lunch and,
when the waiter asked what you wanted said, without much
thought, "Oh, let me have a burger, fries and a soda." Did you
stop and ask yourself what you really wanted or, better yet,
what would be nourishing to your body? Probably not. You
probably ordered something out of habit.

What about at work? Do you keep making the same choices
simply because they are familiar? Imagine for a moment what
would happen if you made some new choices; what if you
ordered a lunch that would really feed your body instead of
weighing it down with high fat, high sugar, high cholesterol

food? Supposing for a moment that at work you made new choices based on what would be more effective, creative or productive. How would that feel? Imagine coming home from work and choosing to spend quality time with your family instead of turning on your TV or surfing the Internet. What about the possibility of making new choices for your work totally? The famous speaker and writer Zig Ziglar has commented that if you go to a job today simply because you went there yesterday, you might want to reconsider your choices.

Rethink

Begin evaluating the choices you make in your daily living. Question whether or not they are guiding you where you want to go. Write in your journal some new choices you could be making and then go and make them. If you are in a financial rut and want to get out, how might you make new choices to accomplish this? What about trading TV time for a new business opportunity? You could begin a part–time business with an investment of a couple of hours each evening and build it into a full time enterprise that could very well provide you with financial independence and wealth.

If you want to lose weight, you could choose to go for a walk rather than eat dessert. Do you want more communication and harmony in your family? Why not model what some families are doing and set aside one evening each week where all family members are present, spending time together talking and sharing their feelings. Some families invite guests and have found the evenings have become a popular social event.

By becoming aware of the choices we make on a daily basis, we can choose those foods, activities and situations that will help us create the kind of life we want and deserve to have. It's the small seemingly insignificant choices we make daily that mold who we become. Your life today is the sum total of the choices you've made up to this point. To change your life, make some new choices.

Conscious choice

Here is a typical scenario that can have a major impact on your health. Suppose you are thirsty. Your first thought is to have a soda. But because you are aware of your choices and act, not just react, you choose a glass of water instead. You could even tell yourself that you'll have the soda after the water if you want. Chances are, the water will have satisfied your thirst and you wouldn't even want the soda. With this one simple distinction, you have made a choice for health and saved a bit of money in the process. Imagine if you took that amount of money every day, or every time you thought about having a soda, and put it into an interest–bearing savings account. Over a period of years you could literally accumulate a small fortune by that one simple action.

These simple daily choices will, over time, help you to have a happier, healthier, more fulfilling life.

COMMITMENT

The one characteristic that separates successful people from the rest of the pack is that successful people are totally committed to their dreams and goals. Successful people don't give up at the first sign of difficulty — they persevere. Successful people don't give into laziness and procrastinate, because they have developed a level of commitment that is stronger than the urge to slack off. How many people do you know who went into a business with all the excitement of a small child on Christmas morning only to quit at the first hurdle? Perhaps you've done this. I know I have. There have been times when I have ventured into a business only to give up at the first hurdle because I had not developed a total commitment to make it work.

Just do it

Several years ago I was considering joining a health club, but when I thought about the upcoming winter I knew I wouldn't want to make this trip several times a week. I had no commitment. Last year, however, I had become tired of not looking and feeling my best. I once again investigated the health club possibility. I had to do something. This time I joined. I set goals and developed a strong commitment to follow through. I knew I had the necessary commitment when one morning at 6 a.m. with the outside temperature below zero, I found myself putting on my workout clothes and going to the club.

I changed

What had changed? All the conditions were the same as before. The only thing that had changed was me. I had developed a strong enough commitment that no matter what, regardless of the weather or any other circumstance, I was going to follow my program. I'm succeeding in attaining better health and becoming more fit because I'm committed. On the following page is a quote from the German philosopher Goethe that demonstrates the power of commitment.

Until one is committed,
there is hesitancy,
the chance to draw back,
always ineffectiveness.

Concerning all acts of initiative
there is one elementary truth,
the ignorance of which kills
countless ideas and endless plans:
That the moment one definitely commits oneself,
then providence moves, too.

All sorts of things occur to help one
that would never otherwise have occurred.
A whole stream of events issues from the decision,
raising in one's favor all manner of
unforeseen incidents and meetings and
material assistance which no man
could have dreamed would come his way.

Whatever you can do or
dream you can, begin it!
Boldness has genius, power,
and magic in it.

JOHANN WOLFGANG VON GOETHE

What About You?

Putting it on the line

At some point you have to be willing to "put it on the line." There is an old saying that if you don't stand for something you'll fall for anything. What do you stand for? Do you have the integrity to hold to your values and commitment no matter what? I believe you do. Whatever your dreams and goals, it's your level of commitment that will make them a reality. Are you willing to continue your effort and not quit? If you are in your own business or planning to enter one, will you risk possible rejection, setbacks and yes, even failure, to pursue your dream? Will you put it all on the line and refuse to give up, no matter what the odds? If you can honestly answer yes to this question, you will greatly increase your chance for success. I would even go so far as to say that all else being equal, the person with the strongest commitment will succeed when all others fail. As the above Goethe quote states "Once you are committed, even providence moves too."

Jimmy, the printer

My friend, Jimmy, left his job to start his own business. When he began, I had asked him how he felt about his new challenge. "I'll give it six months", he replied, "and if it doesn't work, I'll get another job." As you may have already guessed, he went out of business in about four months. Fortunately, the story has a happy ending. He and his wife have started a new venture. They have a new printing business. This time their children are playing in the waiting room and Jimmy's wife, Ann, is doing the typesetting. When I asked him how he felt about the new venture, he said "Great!" He told me they had everything on the line and were going to make it succeed. The last time I visited, they had several employees, had expanded into larger quarters and were running two shifts. Clearly, their level of commitment to the second business has enabled them to build a successful enterprise.

When things don't go the way you want, it's your level of commitment that is tested. If your commitment is strong, you will get through whatever is happening. Whether you're in a new relationship, starting a business, or want to lose a few pounds, the same principle applies. You must be totally committed if you want to succeed.

Burning bridges

Suppose for a moment you want to start your own business. It's a popular practice right now and many people are facing the challenges and reaping the rewards of self employment.

If you're starting a new business, you must get committed to success. In his classic book, *Think and Grow Rich,* Napoleon Hill talks about "burning all your bridges." The reason he suggests burning your bridges is that, if you have no other choice, you will use all of your resources to accomplish what you want. Be careful of the trap of fence sitting. This practice has been the downfall of many well–intentioned people. You must be committed. Remember my friend, Jimmy? When he finally got serious, he succeeded.

Of course, if you can build your business while keeping the security of a regular job and paycheck, by all means do it. There is no point in taking extra risk if you don't have to. Often the husband or wife will keep a job while the other spouse begins the business. This takes some of the pressure off and allows time for the young business to grow and flourish.

Increasing your commitment

How then, can you raise your level of commitment? How will you motivate yourself to take action, even in the face of adversity? What will get you out of bed and exercising on a frigid winter morning instead of pulling the blanket over your head and rolling over? What will drive you to make another sales call even if the last three people turned you down? How will you convince yourself to spend that all-important time with your family when your friends are all going golfing?

Leverage

Your answer will be determined by the amount of leverage you can use to maintain and support your commitment. Let's face it, everything we do is either to gain pleasure or to avoid pain. To develop a strong, powerful and steadfast commitment we need to gain leverage on ourselves. Other people are already using this simple concept to motivate us. Your boss does it by saying something like, "Fred, if you reach the sales quota by January, you'll receive a four percent bonus. You weigh the benefit (pleasure) versus the effect (pain) and decide what you will do. If the pleasure to be gained outweighs the pain or perceived pain, you will do it. If the motivating factor (reward) is big enough, you can accomplish any goal. If I were to ask you to walk 25 miles at night in the pouring rain and offer you $100 as a prize you will probably not even consider doing it. However, if I change the reward and I offer you $100,000 cash to do it, chances are you'll be moving before I finish the sentence.

You will notice that in the highly competitive field of professional selling, the top performers and achievers are rewarded with luxurious prizes for their efforts. This is sometimes a better motivator than even more money.

There are, however, some people who are more motivated by the fear of loss (or pain) than the promise of a reward. However, the principle still holds true.

Children react the same way. If you offer your teens a choice between mowing the lawn and having dessert, or not mowing the lawn and foregoing the dessert you will probably have really tall grass. If on the other hand, you change the outcome for not doing it to being grounded for a week, they will most likely cut the grass. An offer to use the family car for the night might be an even better motivator. Most people respond better to positive motivation.

EXERCISE — COMMITMENT

How do you make the use of this principle of leverage to strengthen your commitment? It's really quite simple. In your journal, write a paragraph or two emphasizing all the benefits you will realize by staying committed and reaching your goal. Really pour it on. Remember, we want to link a lot of pleasure to staying committed. For your business goal, your benefit might be all the things you can buy for yourself and your family with the extra money. List them. It might be the faraway places you can visit and the pleasure you'll experience there. Perhaps it's the extra time you can spend with your loved ones or simply the sense of freedom knowing that you're in charge of your own destiny. Whatever it is for you, write it out.

Agony of defeat

Next, on a new page, write all the pain you will experience if you don't follow through. What will you lose out on? What are you already losing out on by not having reached this goal? What will be the outcome if you don't follow through with your commitments? Maybe it will mean staying stuck in a job you dislike, working for a boss you don't respect, and doing it each and every day for the next 20 years or longer.

Future pace

If you want to gain more commitment to a health goal, ask yourself, "What will I look and feel like in ten, twenty or thirty years if I don't take this action now?" When I did that and saw clearly what my physical condition would be in 30 years if I didn't begin exercising now, it moved me so much I put on a pair of sneakers and went out the door before I even completed the written exercise. That was several years ago, and I have maintained a pretty regular exercise program ever since. When I find myself slipping back into my old, lazy habits (and we all slip once in a while), I only need to repeat this exercise and the motivation and commitment returns. In anything, especially health and exercise, staying focused on a result will help you through the rough spots. Remind yourself *why* you're doing what you're doing.

World class

Do you think Olympic gold medal winners just love to practice? Of course not. I'm sure they would rather do other things during the hundreds of days of practice leading up to an Olympic event, but they stay centered because their focus is on the medal. They see themselves in the winner's circle and see and feel the roar of the crowd. That's what keeps them going through all the hard work it takes to be a world class athlete.

You are a world class person, too.

Stay focused on your result. Use the leverage exercise to help you stay committed to your life and I assure you, you will live a life beyond your wildest imaginations. (Please mark this page, because you'll use this exercise again, after you've completed the chapter about goal setting).

CHAPTER 8 – ACTION

"As the body without the spirit is dead,
so faith without deeds is dead."

JAMES 2:25

Once you've gone through the process of identifying what you want to change in your life, developed new empowering beliefs, made a true commitment to change your life, identified your dreams, become excited about the possibilities that lie ahead, broken through your fears , strengthened your faith and set your goals, the next and most critical step is action.

Do the legwork

As the quote above says, "faith without works is dead."You must be willing to do your part. Your part is to take action — massive action. If you want a big life, take big action.

Focus on results

It's important for us to keep our part in perspective. Our job is to define and set our goals and take appropriate action toward them. Stay focused on your desired result. Leave the details to God. I think we sometimes self-sabotage by trying to control the "how" of getting what we want.

A good example of trying to control the outcome is the story of Linda, a woman in one of my workshops. The first night of the workshop she shared that one of her goals was to go on a vacation. She wrote it down and set a goal to do it. The following week, she shared that her sister was taking her on an all–expense paid trip to Hawaii. When I asked her why she was not excited that her goal came to be in such a short time, she exclaimed that this didn't count because her goal was to pay for it herself. I suggested that she accept the gift graciously and realize she had reached her goal of going on a cruise. The details of how were not her responsibility.

My old car

Once, when I was rebuilding my life after having been at a very low point, I was in a position where I didn't have a car. It wasn't a major problem since I was able to use public transportation, but one of my immediate goals was to obtain a car. I had set it as a goal and went about my business, leaving the rest to God. One night, I was having dinner with my sister, Debbie, and her boyfriend. Out of the blue he said to me, "By the way, I know you need a car, and I happen to have one in a garage. It's not great to look at but it runs well and it's yours for as long as you need it." Did I say, "No, I want to buy my own?" You bet I didn't. I said, "Thank you" and graciously accepted his generous offer.

Stay open to opportunity

Our job is to know what we want and to take action toward it. The details of how and when are in God's hands. In His time, we will have everything we ask for. It's important to remain open to all possibilities and all avenues. If your goal is to increase your wealth and you find a dime on the street, pick it up and give thanks for the increase. Affirm that your wealth is increasing. Don't turn your back on opportunity just because you think you know how life should unfold. You aren't the Creator of the universe. Simply do your part, and everything will work out for your highest good.

Do it now

One of the most important components of the action key is to take an immediate first step. By this I mean that once you have decided upon your goals, look at each one and ask yourself what you can do right now, today, this minute, to begin moving in the direction of reaching this goal. What small, simple action can you take that will start you on your desired path?

For example, if your goal is to get in better physical shape and be more healthy, a simple first action could be to just put on a pair of sneakers and go for a walk. Another might be to make an appointment to go on a tour of a health club.

If one of your goals is to improve your marriage, you could call a florist and send your spouse flowers for no particular reason, other than you love them. You could stop by a travel agency and pick up a brochure for a romantic get-away.

If one of your goals is to be in your own business, you might begin by going to a business opportunity meeting. You could buy a book or two about starting your business. There are dozens of great books about becoming an entrepreneur.

EXERCISE — ACTION

In your journal or goals workbook, make a list of each of your main one–year or short–term goals. Next to each, write one simple action step you will take right away. Then, go and do it.

Action is power

This is a very powerful step for several reasons. First, it signals your subconscious mind that you're serious about this goal. It delivers the message that you're going for it and removes any doubt as to whether this is a real goal or just an empty wish. Next, it brings into play the law of physics that states that a force in motion tends to stay in motion until acted upon by a greater or more powerful outside force. Once you have begun moving on your path, it's likely you will continue. So begin now. An added benefit is the immediate gratification that comes from taking action on your goals. You'll begin to feel a sense of certainty about what you're doing, and this will help motivate you further.

Massive action

It's true that if you want a big life, you need big dreams. It's also true that if you want big results you need to take massive action. Once when I was trying to lose weight but not getting results, I went to a friend who had successfully lost a lot of weight. When I told him that I had been walking for 20 minutes three times a week but not losing weight, he said to me, "How many days are there in a week?" Of course I replied, "Seven." "Then, walk seven days and you'll lose weight." I did it, and it worked. If you're taking action and not getting the results you're looking for, either you're taking incorrect action or you're not taking enough action.

Massive action will produce massive change. Assuming your actions are in the right direction and you are getting a result, you can increase the level of your results by taking more action. Simple, isn't it?

Increasing the odds

For example, if you are making 10 telephone calls each day to prospective customers for your business and succeeding with one or two in getting the appointments that you want, then by making 50 or even 100 calls you will be 5-10 times more successful and produce a 500-1000 percent increase in your business.

Actually, your results will be even better because your massive action will have made you even more proficient in your technique, and your percentage of successful calls will have increased.

If, as in my fitness example, you want to get in better physical shape and are walking 20 minutes, 3 days a week (this amount, by the way, will enable you to maintain your present level of fitness), try increasing this to 30 minutes 5 or 6 times a week. You'll more than double your results.

Have a plan

Simply taking a lot of action, however, will get you nothing but tired and frustrated, unless you have a plan.

In your journal, write each of your major one–year goals on a separate page. Next, write out your action plan. Who will you talk with? What steps will you take? What milestones will you reach along the way? How will you measure your results?

For example, if you're working on a goal to increase your business, you'll list the people you'll be working with. You will brainstorm a list of prospects to call. You will set "mini" goals along the way. Perhaps a mini-goal would be reaching a specific income level from your personal efforts, at which point you will be able to afford additional marketing, like an Internet site, using some of the extra income you earned.

Planning your work

I strongly suggest using some kind of daily/weekly planner. In them are pages for monthly, weekly and daily planning and appointments as well as to do lists, address pages, notes, and other forms to help you become better organized. Use whatever size fits your lifestyle and work habits. I have tried them all and finally settled on the 6 ring size as the best for me. It has always amazed me how many small business people and entrepreneurs don't use a planner. I cannot imagine running my business life without one. Perhaps that's why so many people complain about being too busy and not accomplishing what they want.

Weekly planning

Using your short–term and one–year goals as a guide, you can set weekly "mini goals" — actions you will take that, over time, will move you toward your goals. Personally, I like to take at least a couple of actions each week toward my one year and longer term goals.

> **Tip:** When you are considering an activity, ask yourself, "Will what I'm planning to do bring me closer to or further away from my major goals?" This is a big help in deciding where to invest your time. If you're choosing between watching TV and going to a business meeting, this question will help you remember what's most important for your future.

In addition to your goal oriented actions, your weekly plan can include all of the other things you want to do that week. You might include exercise days, social engagements, meetings, chores, errands, important calls, etc. By using a weekly overview, it's easier to see where in your daily planner these activities can be scheduled.

Priorities and time management

Too many people waste their precious time on what I call "busy work." We have all been guilty of this at one time or another. To avoid unpleasant tasks, we distract ourselves by "majoring in minors." Rather than risk possible rejection and the associated pain, we decide to take some time to get better organized. After all, we rationalize, a person needs to be well organized to succeed. So, off we go to our local office supply store. We carefully shop for colored file folders, labels, business cards & letterhead paper, pens, new software (you'll need a good data base) and an endless supply of other "essentials." This can be a death rattle As my friend, Burke Hedges, always says, "Don't confuse activity with productivity!"

Plan your work; work your plan

It has been proven that a one–hour investment in planning can save you 10 hours of work. That's a 1000 percent return on the time invested. If you interview highly successful people and high achievers, you'll learn that they tend to be well organized. They plan their work and work their plan. If you want to be more successful, learn to plan your activities before you act.

Learn to delegate

Let's face it, no one is great at everything. There will always be tasks and activities in which you excel and there will always be those that are difficult for you. Often, the things we dislike or try to postpone are those things we don't do as well. To really become and remain successful, you must learn to share the responsibility and rewards of your labor. Learn to delegate.

Do what you do best

Dr. Robert Schuller made a brilliant statement that I have integrated into my life. When asked how he was able to accomplish such great feats he said, "I do only those activities that only I can do." What a concept! In other words, if someone else could just as easily do a task, he would delegate it. This freed his time to do those things that required his attention.

In other words, if you do that which only you can do and find others to assist you with the rest, you will accomplish more than if you try, as my wife is fond of saying, "To play all the instruments in the band."

Learned the hard way

This was one lesson I had to learn the hard way and it cost me a great deal, both emotionally and financially. I had been publishing a bimonthly newspaper for small businesses near where I live. It was designed to communicate information which would help businesses grow and prosper. While the idea was sound and the publication well-received for its content, it didn't succeed. I made the (costly) mistake of attempting to do it all myself. I was the editor and publisher, sales person, designer, bookkeeper, and did pretty much everything else except take it to the post office. It became an all-consuming task that took its toll on my health and my life. The day my wife, Georgia, commented that it was "aging me," I ceased publication. She had found the magic word (aging) that would shake me back into reality.

Let set backs be your teacher

I have learned from my mistakes and now publish a new quarterly newsletter for home-based businesses. This time, I have taken Dr. Schuller's advice and included other people. My partner, Julie Parker, loves to sell advertising, a task I would rather postpone. We have others handling various aspects of the publication. Because of my willingness to share the responsibility, this publication is succeeding and I'm enjoying it more because I get to do that which I love doing — namely, writing, editing and working with writers.

Do what you are good at. If you would rather be out selling than doing the accounting, that's fine. Hire a bookkeeper. Surround yourself with a team of capable people and let them do what they do best. Remember the brilliant statement from Zig Ziglar who said, "The way to get what you want in life is to help enough other people get what they want."

Ongoing personal development

Can you really increase your income by simply reading self-help books and listening to tapes or is it just a bunch of hype designed by the people who write and record those books and tapes? Do these principles really work or is it just a lot of "feel good, touchy feely" rubbish? Well, my friend, I can honestly tell you — yes, you can increase your income, and yes, the principles do work! In a moment, I will explain how and why.

Napoleon Hill, in his classic book, *Think and Grow Rich,* James Allen in *As A Man Thinketh,* and Florence Scovel Shinn in *The Game of Life* — all written in the 1920's — taught us we could use the power of our minds to become more successful.

Most of you, especially if you've been in business for a while, have probably been to a seminar on personal development.

Seminars are great. I love going to them, and I really love giving them since it gives me a way to share ideas with a live audience and meet new people, something I really enjoy doing. The problem is, as I'm sure you've experienced, that a week or two after the seminar you are right back into your unproductive habits. You left the seminar all charged up, and once the excitement wore off, you slipped back into your pre-seminar behavior. Reading books and listening to self-help tapes is also a great practice but, like seminars, if it's not done on a *regular* basis it's not nearly as powerful.

Invest in yourself

The key is On-going Personal Development (OPD). The Japanese have a word, *Kaizen,* which means making small daily improvements in every area of your life. It's a principle taught to them by the late W. Edwards Demming who went there, to help them rebuild, after World War II. Since we have no word for this in English, I have chosen OPD, On-going Personal Development as a reminder to follow this formula for success.

It's not so much what you do *sometimes* that makes the difference, it's what you do *daily.* Just as this applies to health and fitness, it applies to success. If you want to succeed and grow, make a daily habit of reading and listening to self-help and inspirational books and tapes. As little as ten minutes each morning can make a major difference. For one thing, you will begin your day on a more positive note and secondly, you will, over time, have assimilated a lot of powerful, positive and thought provoking material.

Proof positive

Several years ago my friend, John DiCicco, came to visit me in my home office. It had been a while since I had seen him so, of course, I asked how he had been. "Great!" he replied, "My income went up more than 15 percent in the last six months." Considering that John is in automobile sales and we were in the middle of the worst recession in decades, I had to learn more. I asked John how he did it and was a bit taken aback when he replied, "I went to a seminar." He went on to explain that the seminar leader suggested reading a self-help book for 15 to 30 minutes a day. John, who had not read a book since high school, bought the speaker's book and began reading every morning before going into the dealership where he worked. He would leave for work a half an hour early each day, sit outside in his car and read the book. That was the only change he made in his daily habits and his income went up 15%, which, in John's case, worked out to be $100 an hour for reading! Would you read 30 minutes a day for $50?

Why this works

It took me a long time to fully understand what had taken place, but it finally "clicked" one day. Imagine John, having just finished his daily ritual of reading an inspirational book, going into the showroom. He is in a positive, uplifted state and is probably cheerful and bouncy. The other salespeople are in the corner, kicking and grumping about the recession. You've seen the scene, everyone stands around complaining about the situation instead of taking action to change it.

Positive energy attracts

You, the new car buyer, enter the showroom. On one side is the group, kicking the coffee pot and looking grumpy. Across the room is John, bouncing around happy as can be. Now, let me ask you the critical question. Who do you want to buy your car from? Who are you most likely to gravitate toward? John, of course. Positive energy attracts people to it.

As a direct result of investing a little time each day on personal development (OPD), John increased his income and felt better in the process. The bonus is that this activity is cumulative. The more you do it, the better you feel.

Success leaves clues

One hundred percent of the self–made millionaires (excluding people in the entertainment field) are committed to reading and listening to self help books and tapes. The most successful direct sales companies have instituted a book/tape of the month program and encourage their people to participate. Amway Corporation, one of the largest, oldest and most successful companies in the world with millions of distributors and billions of dollars in annual sales, teaches distributors to invest time each day reading inspirational and personal development books and listening to tapes.

How many books have you read this month? How many tapes are in your car? Do you think it's a coincidence that companies like Amway, McDonald's, Kodak, Delta Airlines, IBM, AT&T, Century 21, General Motors, Lucent, Marriott, Ford and others have formal employee development programs, using books and tapes, to encourage success in their work force? All you need to do is look at the sales figures for these companies to see the results of these programs.

CHAPTER 9 – SUCCESS TOOLS

"There is no surer way along the road to success that to follow in the footsteps of those who have reached it."

ANONYMOUS

In the following pages are some of the *"tools"* that I, and many others, use to stay on track and condition our minds for a happy and productive life. Use the ones that appeal to you and leave the rest. Play with these and the other examples from this book. Make it fun. Enjoy yourself. Lighten up.

Affirmations

As I mentioned earlier, this is one of the most powerful tools you can use to create change. Recite, write, even sing affirmations about what you want. Be sure to use the present tense (I am, I have, I earn). The Bible talks about the idea that whatever you ask for in prayer, believe you have received it. I believe this is where affirmations fit in. By using affirmations, you are demonstrating your faith in God to provide what you need.

Mirror work

Mirror work is powerful. It puts you face-to-face with yourself and can even be a bit unnerving at first. Stick with it and you will be pleased with the results. Read and recite your affirmations into a mirror while looking at yourself.

Visualization

Sitting quietly and picturing what you want in your life is another powerful tool. Perhaps the most powerful, because it involves more of your senses. While there are several good books written about visualization, it's fairly simple to begin.

Be still and know

Sit quietly in a comfortable place where you won't be disturbed. Relax. Take several deep breaths and become quiet.

When you feel relaxed, simply close your eyes and picture a screen. On this screen, you will project a picture of what you want. Imagine what you want in as much detail as you can. Don't force this, just stay relaxed and see it happen. Use color, sound, smells, and draw upon all of your senses. If, for example, you're picturing your own home, see all of the details of that house. You can put yourself in the picture. See your family there as well. Make it as vivid and bright as you can. Don't strain, simply relax and see the picture.

Invest time in this on a daily basis and you will be amazed at how much it speeds your actually reaching your goals. You need not spend a long time. Five or ten minutes is fine. What you're doing is communicating to your subconscious mind a clear picture of what you want.

When you are finished, let it go. It's now in God's hands. You need to continue to do the leg work, but don't obsess about how this will happen. It just will.

Treasure maps

Treasure maps are another powerful tool that use your visual senses to keep you on track. A treasure map is simply a collection of pictures that represent what you want to have in your life. It can be a simple picture of a new car, or it can be a complex collage that represents your ideal life.

You can include pictures of things you want, places you want to go, and feelings you want to experience. Treasure maps can really be fun. You can draw them, or you can simply cut pictures from magazines, add photos and whatever else you can think of. Place your treasure map where you will see it regularly. Mine, which grew from a simple 11x14 frame to a full 24x36" wall hanging, is in my home office where I see it daily. This is simply another way to stay focused and keep your mind on what matters to you most. You are imprinting your goals on your subconscious mind.

Keeping a journal

One of my mentors, Tony Robbins, once said that, "A life worth living is a life worth recording." Keep a journal of your thoughts, ideas, progress and everything you are experiencing in your life. I have several years worth of journals and it's great to go back and read what my dreams were, say, six or seven years ago. It's a great reinforcement when I realize how many of my goals have been reached. A journal is a wonderful way to record your life. Some people write in their journals every day. Personally, like most things in my life, I do it in moderation.

Your journal is where you will record your dreams and goals, an activity that you will want to do at least twice a year. I usually re–evaluate and do a goal setting exercise at the beginning of the year and on my birthday, which just happens to be in June six months into the year. By all means, invest time on your birthday thinking about your life, your dreams and your goals. This is, perhaps, one of your most powerful days.

Manifestation file

A practice I've begun recently is keeping a file of the things from my treasure map, which I have already received. One day I was removing some pictures from my treasure map because I had already received the items and, rather than throw them away, I put them into a file. At one of my workshops, someone suggested labeling it "my manifestation file" and keeping the pictures of goals that are now a part of my life. This serves to remind me of just how many of my goals and dreams have come to pass.

Gratitude list

One of the ways to remain in a positive state of mind is to develop an attitude of gratitude about your life. Whatever your present condition, there are things you can be grateful for. What about your physical and mental health? Your family and friends? Look around where you live. Consider your possessions, your job. All of those things we tend to take for granted.

Gratitude is one of the major keys to happiness. If you're feeling grateful for what you have, you'll be a happy person. On the other hand, if you're constantly focusing on what you don't have, you will be miserable most of the time. Remember that what you think about tends to expand. If you spend your time thinking about how lucky you are and how grateful you feel, then that will expand as well. Write down all the things in your life you are grateful for, and when you're feeling down take the list out and read it. When you feel grateful, add that to the list. If you can't find anything to be grateful about, go visit someone in a hospital or homeless shelter and compare your problems with theirs.

People I want to meet

Keep a list of the people you would most like to meet. As in goal setting, simply writing it down increases greatly the chance of it happening.

Ideas list

We have ideas all the time. The problem is that most of us either forget about an idea we had, say last week, or we discard it because we think it's of no value, because maybe it was too wild, or we just never act on our ideas. By keeping an ideas list, you eliminate the chance of forgetting what may be a major idea. Some of the most successful businesses in the world were built on the simplest of ideas.

The birth of an ice cream cone

Have you heard about the ice cream vendor at the 1934 World's Fair who, when he ran out of paper cups for his ice cream, borrowed some of those flat, Belgian waffles from the vendor down the way, (who was not selling many anyway), and created what has become accepted worldwide as the ice cream cone? Keep your mind open to new combinations and new possibilities.

Your definite major purpose

If you had all the money you needed and couldn't fail, what is it that you would do? What is it that you are here on earth to accomplish? How can you best invest your time and energy? What is the unique contribution that only you can make to the world? What is important to you? In your journal, write your definite major purpose in as much detail as you can. We are all here to do something. If you are one of those who is fortunate enough, to uncover what that is and willing to go ahead and do it, you'll lead a life beyond your wildest dreams.

YOUR PROMISE TO YOURSELF

"I promise to pursue the dreams God has given me."

DR. ROBERT SCHULLER

Congratulations! You have just taken a major step forward in creating the life you deserve to live. If you skipped over any of the exercises, please go back and do them now. These are some of the "tools" that you can use as you progress in your journey.

Decide now to live your dreams. You have the necessary tools. You have identified what it is you want in your life. Now, it's up to you.

Promise yourself and your family that you will pursue these dreams to the best of your ability. Decide now that you will succeed!

You, and only you, can decide to act. Whatever you want in life, it's there waiting for you. All you need to do is decide what you want and take action and, in the words of Sir Winston Churchill addressing the British troops as they were about to enter combat, "Never, never, never, never give up." Or, on a more positive note:

Always, always, always live your dreams!

CONCLUSION

"I have come that they might have life, and
that they might have it more abundantly."

JOHN 10:10

There you have it. Time tested, proven ideas and techniques you can use to create a life that is beyond your wildest imagination. I know. I've done it. It's now up to you. Are you willing to do the leg work? Are you willing to let go of your old limiting beliefs, change your destructive habits, decide what you really want, put those desires in writing, set goals and have the kind of life that you want and deserve? And finally, are you willing to take the necessary action to accomplish this and create the life that you want? By now, you are well on your way to "designing" the life of your dreams.

If you skipped over any of the exercises, please go back and do them now. Write in your journal regularly, and track your progress. You really can have the life of your dreams. And remember, you have to go for it now because:

This is your life, not a dress rehearsal!

Be well and may God Bless You,

Jim Donovan

ABOUT THE AUTHOR

For more than a decade, Jim Donovan has worked with individuals and companies to help them implement strategies for their personal and professional growth.

Jim's talks & seminars are designed to encourage taking responsibility, identifying your dreams and goals, taking action and achieving results.

His column appears in several magazines, and he is the author of the international bestseller, *Handbook To A Happier Life: A Simple Guide To Creating The Life You've Always Wanted* and *Jim's Jems*, a newsletter for personal and professional development.

Jim's books, articles, seminars and workshops are designed to help people develop strategies for success in their lives.

Jim's core belief is that we *can* create the life of our dreams!